# This is the Way[?]

EPISODE II - REDEFINING A BIBLICAL

COVENANT WAY OF LIFE

## Dr. Will Ryan

CrossLink Publishing

RAPID CITY, SD

Ryan/CrossLink Publishing
1601 Mt Rushmore Rd. Ste 3288
Rapid City, SD 57701
www.CrossLinkPublishing.com

Ordering Information:
Quantity sales. Special discounts are available on quantity purchases by corporations, associations, and others. For details, contact the "Special Sales Department" at the address above.

This is the Way[?]/Dr. Will Ryan. —1st ed.
ISBN 978-1-63357-239-3
Library of Congress Control Number: 2021942504

*To the loves of my life and my inspiration: Krista, Ty, Will, Kade, and Reid.*

*I am also continually in gratitude to my good friend **Matt Mouzakis** co-host of the Expedition 44 YouTube Channel, who researched nearly every topic in this book and co-wrote several sections of it with me.*

# Contents

INTRODUCTION ..................................................... 1

PREFACE ............................................................. 7

CHAPTER 1: The Magi Weren't at the Manger . . .

and a Few Other Problems | Luke 2 ........................ 12

CHAPTER 2: This Is the Way | 1 John 1

and Matthew 28 .................................................. 19

CHAPTER 3: Nephesh Thinking | Deuteronomy 6 .......... 25

CHAPTER 4: Covenant Kingdom Living |

Genesis 2–3 and Revelation 21–22 ........................ 34

CHAPTER 5: The Image of God |

Deuteronomy 26 and Exodus 3 ............................. 39

CHAPTER 6: Who Is Your King? | Deuteronomy 6 .......... 49

CHAPTER 7: The Gospel According to Whom? |

Matthew, Mark, Luke, and John ........................... 56

CHAPTER 8: A Covenant Mission ............................. 63

Chapter 9: Heaven on Earth |

Read Revelation 21 and 2 Peter 3 .......................... 86

Chapter 10: Hell ........................................................ 92

Chapter 11: Final Thoughts: This Is the Way ................... 123

# INTRODUCTION

The goal of this book is to encourage a deeper pursuit of Scripture in the lives of all who faithfully follow Jesus. To truly fall in love with the word of God and therefore, God himself. It sounds simple enough, but many Christians go through life without ever truly developing a love-like relationship and learning to walk with the Father. The great majority of those I have encountered have no construct or understanding of what this means or how to get there, but they continue to desire it. Some pastors today don't have the desire to work through a text to truly seek out what it means within the entire lens of Scripture, and therefore the application falls short. One of the main problems lies therein. If the pastors themselves have a limited framework of the message, how will the congregation get there?

My story is very similar to many others within western church culture. When I was in high school, I responded to an altar call and luckily was assigned someone to "disciple" me. I grew up in a Christian home, and even previous to my decision, I was already speaking a lot of the "church language." I followed the way that had been set before me and attended one of the greatest mainstream Bible colleges of our time, often referred to as the Harvard of Bible colleges. I took great pride in my stride as a card-carrying Christian. With most all of the answers systematically rehearsed and memorized, I rose to the top; I planted a couple of churches and started more Christian programs than I can count, all within the framework of the "great American church." In other words, I had become well indoctrinated into what I thought was the right way. I found myself happily checking off the boxes of my Christian portfolio. Looking back, I have to admit, most of this felt really great to me; I fully accepted and even excelled at all of it. Many aspects of my Christian life followed the biblical models, but something just wasn't there. I wanted to "Love" but didn't truly love.

One of the most difficult facets of life is to try to see through the eyes of Christ. Often, we become so immersed in the American way that it becomes difficult to clearly see the way things really are within a spiritual framework. Everyone following a path usually thinks or hopes that they are on the "right" path. Nothing in my life necessarily imploded or blew up. I was blessed that, for the most part, my life was very smooth, comfortable, and even happy. In fact, it felt very much like I was living the American dream. I had experienced God's love but didn't really know how to love back. I was missing a big part of the recipe.

Many before me have been on a similar path and have had something trigger a change of course. For me, it happened when I started learning the biblical languages as part of my corporate church climb. As I started to learn the basis of interpreting the biblical languages, I found that my exegesis was sloppy, despite attending a Bible college and majoring in the Bible. It felt as if I had dived deeply into Scripture for the first time, and what I found was amazing love. You see, I had never really fallen in love with Scripture before. It was simply a means to an end for me. As I started practicing my newfound languages, I found myself not loving the languages themselves, but rather learning to love the text. Something magical took place: as I learned to love the Word, I learned to love Jesus.

As I continued to be filled by the Word deeply working through me, I found that much of the way things had always been presented to me really didn't add up. I was always afraid to challenge the great questions of the Bible, as if I might not find the answers or worse, find the wrong answers. I had always believed that the inspired Word of God completely agrees with itself, but I hadn't experienced it and had very little confidence in putting that puzzle together. For the first time, I got brave. As I worked through every text and doctrine, it became like a magnet drawing me closer to Jesus. The mysterious way that this love story fit together within the entire lens of Scripture began to fill me with something that had always been missing.

I became enthralled with my newfound love for Scripture and exegesis (critical interpretation of the text). Over and over, I began to realize that the systematic understanding that I had not only accepted but had become a poster child for seemed like it required a great amount of working through—what I now refer to as theological gymnastics. It wasn't that I was previously blinded to these things, it was just that I was more interested in sounding like I knew all the answers than I was in actually trying to find the truth. It wasn't an expedition of love as much as trying to be "right." As I started understanding what had to take place within the text to put together a certain accepted theology, I become more aware of the problems that persisted within those ideological frameworks. How had I missed this for the better part of thirty years? As I continued to listen to the Spirit and dive into the context of Scripture, my experiences in the traditional American church often seemed far from what I found the biblical descriptions of living with Jesus as the Lord of my life to look like.

As a "type-A" analytical (and I get that not everyone has to or wants to think this way), I find that biblical theology within the context and lens of the entire biblical narrative is empirical within any Christian teaching. Without Scripture driving what we do, we have an empty view of the message, and in the end, what we are trying to accomplish may actually drive some further from the truth than closer to it. Unfortunately, I have seen and even been a part of too many churches preaching an American-style gospel that is void and problematic, leaving people aimlessly wandering within a fairy tale of church cheerleading.

Many have been taught a denominational perspective or theological view without realizing or researching other viable options within Scripture. Because of this, let's just put the labels aside and take a fresh look at what the Bible says. This book will be theological, but will intentionally drop the typical theological terminology or jargon other than to make associations when needed.

Let me give you a simple example of how I have learned to explore the text. In Romans 11:26 Paul says, "All Israel will be saved." I often allude to this phrase as simply referring to all those who will, in the end, find their place in the presence of God in eternity. Seems simple enough right? Most everyone will agree with this statement. Yet many "theologies" seek to bend it to mean things it simply doesn't say within the text. You might be surprised to find that there are at least four definitive views on this verse with all kinds of theological labels. We could also have a conversation on the terminology of God's people throughout Scripture and how each is used differently or the same— words like Israel, Hebrew, Jews, the elect, the church, and many other similar terms. Some doctrines and denominations even seek to make their own versions of the Bible by carefully changing words to try to fit their narrative. I have also found it helpful to could look at Second Temple literature to try to gain an understanding of what other authors of the time meant when they used the same terms. We could even find out why different denominations or theological camps choose to interpret this verse differently, and determine what other theology has bearing on their understanding of this verse. Is it related to anything else within the Bible or doctrine? Does the language it was written in affect the interpretation? How do scholars understand this passage and why? But perhaps the most important element of interpretation is simply thinking through the passages at hand as you call on the power of the Holy Spirit for clarity, discernment, and application to your life. We will often quickly take someone else's view, thinking they must be much more intelligent than we are, and in the process fall short of letting our minds and hearts be blessed by the working-through process. This, I have found, is the path to falling in love with the Word.

I don't think most authors intentionally lead anyone astray, but when writers interpret a text, I often wonder what their defining reasoning is. Do they understand the biblical and theological implications?

Do they necessarily know that to take a view like they have means cutting up a text and interpreting it differently than what is commonly acceptable within hermeneutics? Do they know that what they are doing with the text to make fit into their framework is problematic, but they continue anyway because the view has been tied to them or to those in their "camp"?

Have you ever felt like the author or the preacher is hiding something? When a pastor just throws a difficult part of the Bible out there and doesn't spend time making sense of it, it becomes problematic and can have lasting effects. Not only have pastors nearly completely lost the emphasis of scholarly pursuit for the Word, but they have failed even more by not shepherding their flocks in that pursuit, which is the preeminent calling of a pastor.

I've heard many pastors do this—for instance, reading over how Abraham was asked to sacrifice his son to God. To nearly everyone in our culture this story just sounds bizarre. There are several tough passages such as this in the Bible, and thousands of years later, we have a hard time reconciling them with the culture in which we live. It is important to know that Scripture can stand alone, for itself—and it will. But what God asks some of his people is for us to dive into Scripture to help others understand it. If you take Scriptures like this one in the context they were written and work through understanding them, there are logical answers (and usually more than one). It is also likely that these passages would not have come off so strangely in their original culture, but now, thousands of years later, they are often the texts that make people want to walk away from the church. I am convinced that everything within the Bible makes sense in the complete lens of Scripture and that it all agrees with itself. Part of what we are called to do is to figure out *how* it agrees. Too many people are afraid that they're going to unravel something that just doesn't work, and they don't trust Scripture (or God) enough to work through it. Jesus is the Word, and the word is greater than that!

Too many people lose the fervency of faith because they never fall in love with the Word. They have simply stopped exploring the mystery of Scripture and have never experienced the all-encompassing love of the message. Unfortunately, I have found that most of my best conversations concerning unbiased Christianity take place far from the walls of church. In fact, a lot of times they happen in places that most would consider to be polar opposites of church.

My heart is to show those entangled in the American/Western cultural church a better mosaic of being captivated by the Word, allowing them to find a better walk with Jesus—to see that starts as work will soon become the love of their lives.

Some of my favorite authors are ones whose biblical perspectives changed a little bit in an honest pursuit of scriptural exegesis. I want to know why. At any rate, you might occasionally read something (even within this book) that you'll question, and you should question it. That's why I have provided a fair amount of extra material and homework for those of you who want to dive in and understand how I arrived at the conclusions that I have. You may or may not land where I have, but as a result I bet you will find Jesus! I hope that this process impacts you the same way it has impacted me, and that as a result you find yourself falling in love with the word of God over and over and through and through.

Am I claiming to have it all figured out? Absolutely not. For me it's a lifelong journey, and I pray every day that God may continue to bring clarity to my heart, soul, and mind—and to those I teach.

# PREFACE

Originally, what motivated me to pen my thoughts was the covenant of marriage. I am regularly asked to marry people, and I often find that those couples don't understand the basic relationship that God seeks with his people, and therefore, certainly can't understand what covenant-living with each other looks like. Upon desiring to counsel a couple, I found myself needing to first debunk some pretty horrific notions they held about God and the church. I regularly thought, "How have we (the church) gotten this far away from the primary message of the Word of God?" My original goal was to write a book that established a scriptural understanding of the Bible before talking about marriage specifically. By chapter five or six, it became very apparent to me that I wasn't just writing a guide for couples to start their marriages, but possibly a method of understanding that might give spiritual meaning to the masses.

The purpose of this book is to gain a better understanding of theology within life and therefore begin to experience a reciprocal loving relationship with God. The goal is a return to biblical thinking rather than relying on tradition or simply accepting views you might have always thought were based in the Bible. Put simply, the Bible is a story of God's love relationship with his people. This is based on covenants.

This book takes aim at explaining some deeper theological thinking, but at the same time keeps it simple. There will be theological questions that I am not going to answer in the book. That journey is for you, and

I pray that this book may ignite it, but not complete it. The chapters are linked to theological YouTube discussions that will show Scriptures and explain the biblical theology behind each chapter. The book is designed to give you an option of investing as much or as little time as you can. You can read the Scriptures and introductory quotes given for each chapter and watch the longer films suggested by searching the keywords on my YouTube channel (go to YouTube and search for "expedition44"). Once you are in the channel, click the search icon and type in the keyword given for each chapter. In many cases you will see several videos that match the chapter content.

You will find that this book is centered around textures of exegetical interpretation. The goal of any hermeneutic is to find the meaning as the (inspired) writer intended. To do this we need to read within context. This means the surrounding verses, the entire book, and the meaning within the complete lens of Scripture. We also need to seek to understand the cultural context. The Old Testament needs to be understood in its Ancient Near Eastern context; the New Testament needs to be approached from a Jewish mindset within a Greco-Roman context to give clarity to the message of the Old Testament. We have the luxury of reading both many years later, allowing us to see much more of the whole picture than the original writers (of the Old Testament especially) were given. But at the same time, we need to realize that even though the entire work is written for us and there is much to glean from it, the majority of the message was written to a specific group or person that we are not a part of. Many people seek to find a literal interpretation of Scripture. Unfortunately, oftentimes the most literal meaning of a word doesn't make sense to us or in our language. The best interpretation of the word may be metaphorical or symbolic. We often don't have the same understanding of the original culture that would have been implicit in the wording of the original languages. To give you an example, we have one word for prayer in English. There are two in Greek and more than a dozen in Hebrew, and these meanings shift depending on time period and cultural dynamics. We aren't simply translating languages, but translating cultures. This has become a fundamental flaw within our American interpretive thinking. We want to read an American understanding into the cultural narrative of the Bible, and it simply doesn't work. It gives the text a completely different sensibility than that of the context and culture it was given to. We need to train ourselves to look at the totality of Scripture for the best form of interpretation.

I often hear concerns about reading extrabiblical sources, especially the ones contained in Catholic Bibles. Many get hung up on the thought of inspiration. This is a topic that needs to be carefully approached. But many of these extrabiblical sources, especially ones written within the Second Temple period, give us great insight to the way people were thinking about biblical things. They aren't always right and certainly are not to be approached as inerrant Scripture, but rather as a social commentary. The ancient writer likely had a worldview far closer to that of the Scriptures than what we have today. If you read books written today that share theological opinions on Scripture, why wouldn't you read opinions from others that held a closer cognitive frame of reference to the biblical authors? How did they think about Scripture? Unfortunately, most readers of the Bible today are filtering the message through a traditional understanding that was handed down to them and likely has little to do with the real exegesis of Scripture. Even worse are the doctrines that knowingly use certain verses as proof for a denominational understanding that is supposed to be within the pages of the Bible. This "slicing and dicing" method has become the norm within the context of most sermons today, and pastors have become so accepting of this practice themselves that the call to study Scripture has become almost completely lost from the church. I have been to so many "Bible studies" that were far from studying what Scripture actually says.

What I have experienced throughout my life in Christianity is that there is a dedicated group within the church that wants to sincerely know and follow the way of the Lord. Most of them think that what they have been traditionally taught is the only way things might exist or be possible within Scripture. They want to stand strong and represent biblical truth. The problem comes when people find themselves clinging to what they have always been *told* Scripture says rather than examining and testing for themselves what Scripture actually says. Some will even tell you that to approach Scripture with such an unbiased method is dangerous. That you may be swept away into heresy. I have found that many people think they know the way, but if they approach their studies in prayerful pursuit of truth, they may find that what they have been traditionally taught could be farther from biblical truth than they ever imagined. What does the Bible actually say? What is the true way of life for the allegiant believer?

What investment will you make? You can simply read each chapter and pray or spend the better part of a week on each chapter by looking up the passages and reading through them slowly, asking some key questions for each set of passages, and then watching some videos on the chapter content and discussing them in prayerful consideration with your spiritual family. I would also recommend reading the books I quote from at the beginning of each chapter if you want a thorough understanding of the chapter's content and a more in-depth (and likely scholarly) pursuit of the topics mentioned.

- These are some good consideration questions to ask for each Scripture reading:
- What have you always thought this text meant? How does it compare to what it actually says? Consider any presuppositions and pre-understandings that you have brought with you upon reading the text.
- How could this story or message have been influenced by the culture it was written compared to the application of it within our life and culture today?
- Does the interpretation of any of the words from the original text (exegesis and grammar) have a significant impact on what this means to you?
- Consider the fourfold sense of biblical hermeneutics: literal, moral, allegorical (spiritual), and anagogical (you may need to watch the X44 videos on hermeneutics first to best understand these textures of interpretation).

I hope you enjoy the journey and that you are deeply blessed within both your spiritual family and your relationship with the Father. The greatest goal of this book is that you find a passion for the sacred way of life and a begin a journey to deeply know God and the Word. That you may truly fall in love as you walk with him.

—Dr. Will Ryan
**YouTube Expedition44 keyword search: hermeneutics exegesis**

CHAPTER 1

---

# The Magi Weren't at the Manger . . . and a Few Other Problems | Luke 2

Our Christmas creche sets remain as they are because "ox and ass before him bow for he is in the manger now." But that manger was in a warm and friendly home, not in a cold and lonely stable. Looking at the story in this light strips away layers of mythology that have built up around it. Jesus was born in a simple two room village home such as the Middle East has known for at least three thousand years. Yes, we must rewrite our Christmas plays, but in rewriting them the story is enriched, not cheapened.

—Kenneth Bailey, *Jesus Through Middle Eastern Eyes*

I love Christmas. I love Christmas for a lot of reasons but perhaps the top of my list is because it is the one time when nearly everyone, regardless of their backgrounds, beliefs, and ideals, is open to, and at least partially embraces, a biblical story. The problem is, the story we wish to embrace in our Western, American civilization is actually pretty far from the reality of Scripture. Is this a problem?

Some Christians have recognized this, but others haven't considered it much. So, as much as I love that the "world" is open to a story of the coming Messiah two thousand years ago, I am also hesitant to fully embrace the idea because of the many inaccuracies that come with it. To me it seems a little crazy that nearly every church embraces the world's fallacious version of Christmas. Some Christians have chosen not to celebrate, but I am not convinced of that kind of thinking either; we might be missing a God-given opportunity.

Is the world's nativity story really that bad? Well, any time we approach Scripture I think it is important to get the truth from the passage. Many have given their life to this pursuit. We get to know the Word, and the Word was and is God. Not only that, but our core directive or calling as a follower of Christ is to disciple. It is a journey—and after all, that is the central theme and idea of receiving the good news. The question then becomes, what good is it if it's wrong? Every year in December, we join the world in the joy of the nativity story, where three kings come to a stable and visit a fair-skinned, American-looking family with a baby wrapped in straw and cuddled up in blankets in an open-air, barely roofed stable, surrounded by animals. I could write a complete work on this (and maybe I should—later) but many have attempted something similar; that isn't the goal of this writing. Let me explain why and how this relates to all of us.

First, let's get the main elements of the story right. We all know that there was no room for them in the inn. Nearly every American has this part of Luke 2:7 memorized. Surprisingly to many, we don't really have the word translated "inn" (*katalymati* in Greek) in English. Why? Because it isn't within our culture. You see, languages and stories are defined by the socio-cultural atmosphere of the places of their origin. If we travelled back to this Greco-Roman time when everyone traveled to their hometown for a national census, we might find a very different idea of an inn. It wasn't a hotel, although many "inns" seemed to be something similar during a census and that's why this may seem confusing to us. It wasn't even a hitching post for the animals. It was more personal: it was the lower room. I love the use of opposites in

Scripture; when it's put this way, you may see the significance of how Christ entered through the lower room and exited the world following a covenant made in the upper room. The lower rooms were where the work got done—the washing of dirt, grit, and grime. This represented the heart of the home. Some people had really nice homes even back then, but the lower room did not reflect it. Most homes in Bethlehem could neither afford nor make space for a stable, so at night animals (the prized assets of the culture) were brought inside to be safe from bandits.

No matter how nice the home was, if a baby were to be born, guess where that kind of messy delivery would have taken place? We might also consider a "replacement" comparison: if something new has more value than all of your other assets, there may not be room in your "inn" for both. Do you want the world and all its assets or Jesus in your work room? Since the home was the center of life, this is a beautiful picture of Christ occupying your heart and living as light within every godly person.

From a young age, I had the image of Mary on a donkey being dragged into Bethlehem by Joseph while he knocked on every door asking for a place to stay. I remember thinking, "What kind of loser was Joseph?" Couldn't he have planned ahead for his poor pregnant wife or girlfriend or whatever she was (this is another discussion though)? Perhaps he didn't plan on going to the census—perhaps he wanted to hide her away or something. There may be some accuracy to that, but most likely the house would have belonged to family, and they would have been ready for Mary and Joseph. The idea of an irresponsible Joseph isn't represented in Scripture. Theologically, we always need to ask what makes the most sense to believe and how does it fit the cultural thinking of the day. This approach (or texture of interpretation) is called the socio-rhetorical hermeneutic.

What about the famous Christmas carol "Away in a Manger?" It says, "The cattle were lowing." This nineteenth century hymn, widely accepted by the church, continues to share a more fairy-tale version of the story than we get from the Bible—and everyone, devout Christians and the world alike, joins in on the fairy-tale version. Most people know more about what they think the biblical narrative says through these songs and Christmas plays than they do from the actual biblical text.

Then we have "We Three Kings." This is one of my favorite parts of the story. What we know from Scripture is more detailed than what people typically think, especially when you read the New Testament together in context with the Old Testament. Too often we miss this by separating the testaments. The Bible tells us about the Magi from the east. The word *magi* is often translated as "wise men." We make that out to mean "kings," and we find that that may not be far off. Who are these men? If you look at the biblical narrative as a complete story, you'll notice a few clues.

To do this we will need to back up a bit before moving forward. This circular way of understanding is central to Scripture and you actually might have missed it despite spending your entire life in church, so let's have this quick conversation. It goes like this: God wants to be with his creation and walk with them. It starts this way in the garden of Eden and then gets messed up by the Satan/snake figure resulting in man being cast out from the garden (or, the sacred temple that God gave Adam and Eve to be with him in his presence). From there, man continually chooses (out of free will) to follow something or someone other than God. We discover a reoccurring downward spiral of humankind walking away from God. This is the heart of the story. It is a story of a God who is faithful and continues to make covenant promises with those he loves, while those he loves keep breaking the promise. Man and woman keep walking farther away from God. What does God deeply desire? That man and woman, in free will, would choose to love him back and have a deep and intimate covenant relationship with him, walking with God and in essence bringing back glory to him. This covenant relationship is based on love and intimate knowledge, and it is not only what God wants between us and himself, but also for all humankind amongst each other through the sacred covenants.

The Bible is a story of how God created an environment to walk with humankind. The central story is that it gets mucked up and that God loves us enough to work through the hardship and formulate a divine plan (or set of dynamic plans) to bring it back to its original design.

Over and over, we fall short in this covenant relationship: Noah and the flood; Abraham and his direct offspring; and of course the Israelites who eventually fall into captivity, exile, and the diaspora (that is, being spread out). So, what about the "Three Kings"? Well, the kings might actually be the main connection between the old and new stories. Israel continually failed in its covenant with God to the point that God essentially divorced them into captivity and exile in judgment. But he still had a plan, and he upheld his part of the promise by using the faithful remnant of Israel, grafted with a seed of the gentiles, to bring forth the Messiah. The Messiah reveals to us that he isn't just the answer the Jews were looking for, but the rest of the world as well. This is essentially the good news.

Do you remember the story of Daniel? Who is he in charge of? Yes, the wisest men. And where is Babylon in proximity to Bethlehem? East. For now, I will just leave this here; I think you can make the connection. Am I saying that the magi were God fearing men? Maybe, but no, we don't have that. We often even call them astrologers, which implies more of the opposite connotation. But judging from their gifts they knew this was the prophecy foretold in the Scriptures. Their gifts showed that they understood the significance of the coming King. Gold was a symbol of royalty and often meant virtue. Frankincense was a symbol of deity and represented another dimension associated with prayer to the spiritual world. Myrrh seems odd at first, as it was an embalming fluid of oil and during ancient days represented suffering—isn't that amazing! As you can see, there were a lot of prophetic, messianic messages in the magi's gifts. However, getting back to the story, we don't know exactly when or how the star appeared. It is possible the magi saw the star significantly before the Messiah was born. Maybe, but again we don't know for sure. Hermeneutically it is implied that some time went by before the magi visited. We know this by the use of specific language that describes Jesus as a child when the Scripture previously used the word for "baby." The location is also likely different, but that doesn't really influence much of the narrative. My point is, as good as the magi look in your front yard nativity scene . . . they weren't at the manger. There are a lot of reasons for this, but I will leave that on your own research.

Then we have the complexion problems. I think most people in America like the picture of white Jesus. In fact, it has been said by some that this idea has inadvertently damaged the church and given way to feelings of racism making walls within religion. The Bible actually does not speak on details of Christ's complexion, but we know his genealogy and can say without too much problem he wasn't the white Jesus that America (or even Roman Catholic Europe) has painted him to be. He more likely had dark skin, dark hair, and dark eyes.

What about the date? I bet you have heard that our modern date for Christmas, December 25, was chosen in an effort to "Christianize" a pagan holiday. Well, there is some truth to that. You may have also heard that March 25 is a more viable date, or even January 6. I will simply say this and leave the rest to you: I can say virtually without any doubt that Jesus was not born on December 25.

By now you're probably making several connections, but still there is the main question: What does the fabricated nativity scene have to do with your way of life and how it relates to godly living? Year after year Christians learn a lot of the things I have mentioned, but they continue to go along with the popular depiction. Isn't that strange? Consider this same principle at work: What if you found out that something that you had been doing year after year simply wasn't true? We have words for this, including propaganda, fairy tales, lore, and even flat out lies. Doesn't the Bible teach that we should be honest and truthful? By mindlessly going along with the "world" every year in celebrating this version of one of the most holy aspects of history we lose truth and integrity. At face value it may seem the stakes are low. Donkeys, stables, magi . . . what does it really matter, right? Some may say that these are just subtle inaccuracies and frankly might think history is likely filled with them; no one really knows what the culture was genuinely like or exactly what happened. Perhaps you think every written account is slightly stretched. That's one of the problems of our American Christian culture and perhaps a major problem with Christianity in the world. We are too quick to let the world infiltrate biblical truth, and even our pastors and churches become complacently fine with it.

As easily as we continue to go along with a fairy-tale Christmas story, we continue to let the world be the measure of truth, especially as it applies to our relationships. We have given way to the powers of the rulers and principalities of the world, allowing them to challenge truth all the way to the core of what we believe: the story of the Messiah.

Today I want you to consider something. A covenant, a pledge, a rekindling of truth in your life. Let's start simple. Pray with me that the Spirit will reveal what is biblical truth in your life and that you might start to be convicted to uphold this within your relationships with God and with the family of God. Involve someone else: your spouse, your family, or maybe a group from church (I refer to this as your spiritual family). This journey is best experienced with brothers and sisters in Christ. Begin to read Scripture regularly and with a fresh approach. This is a big prayer. Start making baby steps, but eventually this will require complete honesty and openness. Nothing is a secret. This is going to take some time between you and God as you start talking intimately and getting to "know" each other—possibly for the first time—as you fall in love with the Word. That is what it means to be one in the Spirit which is also truth. giving of the heart, mind, and soul; think big, *nephesh* living.

*YouTube Expedition44 keyword search: Christmas story*

CHAPTER 2

# This Is the Way | 1 John 1 and Matthew 28

For thirty-four years I've studied the Gospels and have come to these three convictions:

1. Jesus didn't define the Christian life the way that I did and the way many do today.
2. Jesus defined being a Christian as "following" Him.
3. Following Jesus is bigger than the single-moment act of accepting Christ

But what does this [following Jesus] look like? . . . the Bible reading, praying, going to church, evangelizing approach is not enough. I'm going to suggest that Jesus focused on other things and as we do the same, each of these other items takes its place as a means to Jesus' bigger ideas. Instead of personal practices of piety, Jesus offers us a kingdom-holiness plan. Jesus offers us a kingdom dream that can transform us to the very core of our being. His vision is so big we are called to give our entire lives to it. His vision is so big it swallows up our dreams.

—Scot McKnight, *One.Life*

What if I told you that you (and we can even say your friends or family) were chosen to go on a trip with other friends and that the cost was paid for. Would you go? To most people all I would really need to say is something like "paid in full" coupled with Bora Bora, Cabo, or Kauai and that would be enough. I bet I had you at "free"! In fact, I bet you would put up with a lot if I held up to that part of the deal. But let's say I ask for more than that. I want you to simply have faith and trust me throughout this whole trip. I want to know that you're going to be faithful to me and your spiritual family in every way. I expect you to stay with me and follow me for the entire trip. There will be times when things may not seem great and you're not going to understand why (you might be tempted to think your way could be better, or tempted by the ways of others to begin thinking their path is better). You're not going to know what is going on sometimes or be given the whole story, but I have it, so I am asking for your complete and utter trust. Could and would you do that? I bet you would—it still sounds great right? We're all getting on the plane?

Let me continue: I want you to give me your absolute best, every-thing you are, every skill you have, whether you know it or not. You're going to be asked to use the gifts you have been given. You may have to get out of your comfort zone to discover strengths that you have and didn't realize were within you. Could and would you do that? I bet you would.

Even when times get difficult, I need you to stay with me . . . don't give your allegiance to anyone else along the way. Put your pride aside and work with each other, respecting that in this covenant we are bet-ter together. Be committed to our group, be accountable to each other. If something gets between you, work it out before the sun goes down (I can help you with that). Cover each other and be encouraging in ev-ery way. Go out of your way to put others first. Be humble and lead by example as you mentor those beside you and be open to learning from everyone around you. Be mentored yourself.

To most of you those things sound okay, right, maybe even really great, like a breath of fresh air. We all know that even on the best trip, things may not be ideal and might get tough, yet we sort of welcome times like this. Deep down, that thinking is built into every human. In the core of who we are, we understand that often great things take work, and as we commit to this and invest in it, we innately desire these situations in our lives. We want to be hardy workers who are found faithful, allowing us to be used to our full potential. We want to be part of something great that surpasses the menial.

In many ways, I bet you think this trip sounds amazing, almost unreal. Perhaps a chance to experience the best thing you have ever known. I am sure by now you are putting together that this is a figurative description of our calling. God wants us to walk with him. This "trip" is a picture of discipleship. That is the major thrust of who God is calling us to be, both for him and his kingdom.

We want this life, but we often lose sight of it. We lose sight because things get in the way and we don't prioritize. We let others down and they let us down. We lose sight because it gets hard and we don't see the payoff. We don't learn to really love. We grow weary and let things start to compromise our system.

What if we didn't? What if we held true to our mission for the entire "trip"? Unfortunately, we often think this cannot be done. We give in to allowing ourselves to fall short because everyone else is. We fail to hold up our bargain to not only be this person, but also to help others to be this person.

We let the world replace godly principles and missional thinking with whatever it is tempting us with. If we could only see ourselves from God's perspective, I bet we would look so weak. Yet he desires to be our strength. From the very beginning, God created a sacred environment for us to partner with him. His deepest desire is to simply walk with us. Think about this for a moment. The greats like Enoch, Noah, and Abraham all walked with God. When God called his chosen people, Israel, what did he desire? To tabernacle with them. To walk in sacred living, in a sacred space, in a sacred land with people fully committed to him and this way of sacred life.

In the New Testament, it seems that things haven't changed much. John says that if we claim to be in Christ, we must *walk* as he did. The Greek verb *peripateo* had its roots in the Hebrew way of thinking. Sometimes we say we want to know what the Bible literally says, but often what it literally says is based upon the culture and the lives of those by which it was written. Many times, the Scriptures communicate as much metaphorically as they do literally. The best translation may not be the exact word, but the meanings of the word. You see, when John used this word, he was depicting the Hebrew word *halach*, which was commonly used to describe a way of life. In Hebrew, words are often related. You will notice the likeness: *halach* is very closely related to *yalak*, which means "to go." And from there we also have *mahalak*, which means "journey." So, when we put these similar Hebrew words together, we better understand what John was saying. That we are called "to go" and be deeply committed to this sort of missional sacred thinking, which is, in its very essence, the calling of life: a journey. What God desires most is for us to walk with him. This is his way of life for us. Perhaps this is a new way of understanding and applying Matthew 28 in your life.

But there is still more implication to what John is saying. When he employed this Hebrew idiom, it also implied a sense of community that was built into the Yahweh (Yahweh is the actual Hebrew name of God) culture. Every God-fearing Jew would have understood something more here: that this is not just a self-centered journey. It doesn't just encompass you, like we often think in our American culture; it also involves a responsibility for and with others. We need to love God but also love our neighbor. We need to be right ourselves with God, but also be right with others. Remember the story of Achan and the sin in the camp in Joshua 7–9? We all know what that meant, but we fail to embrace this philosophy in our own lives. We have written it off as cultural change. Yet this has been God's way of right thinking from the very beginning, and it did not change from one testament to the other.

Consider this verse: "Let each of us please his neighbor for his good, to his edification" (Romans 15:2 NASB).

There is a certain paradigm within a "Jesus culture." The world can't make sense of the allegiant conviction of a Christian, and the world isn't often allured by the narrow road of Christian ideals. To both sides, the other is countercultural or backwards in thinking. To those fully invested in the kingdom and the seemingly backwards logic (to the world) of Jesus that states "the first shall be last," biblical paradigms can help us make sense of a dark, mucked up world.

Paul and Jesus both claimed to continue living by the law yet preached that it was no longer "necessary," yet we should also "follow Jesus's example." Most Christians have no idea what that law was or meant, and to an extent that is okay. If you practice what Jesus teaches, you're following it anyway.

Paul speaks to this when he says, "Let each of us please his neighbor." This should be read in the context of rabbinical Jewish thought of the Second Temple period, tempered by the teachings of Jesus. The Greek verb *aresko* implies creating a "line" of positive relationship. It is the idea of muscle memory through repetitive action. It is an old-covenant way of thinking usingwords like "make peace," "reconcile," and "stand," by as forms of literary device such as reiteration.

Jesus taught that we are to deny ourselves in order to please or serve others. This is the calling of humble servants to the kingdom. When read in context, the following verses go on to tell us that "whatever was written" continues to infer the law. We have been given an outline to follow. In the New Testament it is clear that this shouldn't be a legalistic set of laws (it's about the heart) but that the law still should be considered. Everywhere you look, the New Testament proclaims the same message as the Old Testament law.

In the Old Testament you were in covenant with fellow believers. It was communal thinking. You went to war for a brother because your blood was the same as theirs; it didn't even matter so much whether you agreed with the fight, you had his back.

Today, believers still need to think in this kind of Old Testament value system. If your brother is getting stoned, you step in and draw the line. As a body of believers, let's take back this kind of ancient-covenant Jesus thinking. There are a few lines that need to get drawn and redrawn.

Today I ask you to consider this journey, the way God designed you to live for him. The walk might seem really hard at first, but let's remember those small steps. One foot in front of the other and eventually we can climb this mountain together. I want you to consider this way of life with your spiritual family and I urge you to consider this covenant of commitment to the ancient sacred way of living. The world wants you to think there are better options, or that this way is too hard to be followed. But deep down in the core of who we are, we know that this is the way of the Father and that it has been given to us as life: life complete, life eternal, and life to its fullest.

*YouTube Expedition44 keyword search: Walking*

CHAPTER 3

# Nephesh Thinking | Deuteronomy 6

Jesus' call for each of us to surrender to Him—personally, mentally, physically—when sifted through the Jesus Creed [Matthew 22:37–40], reveals what surrender really is: a total expression of love. The white-flag prayer that Christians utter each day, "May your will be done," is a white flag that speaks of a total love for God (by following Jesus) and for others. Surrendering ourselves to God is not giving up things for God so much as giving ourselves to God.

—Scot McKnight, *The Jesus Creed*

One of the core concepts of the Bible is that God has given us all that we have and all that we are, and he desires that we give that back to him. In the Bible this is referred to as *first fruits*; I will dive more into this later. Throughout this book you are going to see me keep referring to the problem of a westernized way of thinking. The Eastern world (in which the Bible was written) thinks as a whole: we are all responsible in part for the journey of the whole community. It's the concept of loving God and your neighbor. The Western world thinks just in terms of *me*. This is what the last chapter introduced. To continue our dilemma, we then compound this thought pattern with even more "American" thinking. I don't mean this to be negative in any way toward America; it is simply the culture that most people reading this find familiar. We have been given whatever we want. In many ways we have become our own gods and hardly feel that we need the one true God in our lives.

We as a Christian whole have become scripturally complacent. Church tradition likely defines your understanding of biblical doctrines and concepts better than Scripture itself. The church seems to have accepted a watered-down view of covenant living. Pulpits have become a place for cheerleading the most basic elements of Scripture. The majority of the church are baby Christians in terms of their knowledge of the Word. We have gotten so far away from the basic thrust of what the gospel is and equated it with what the gospel isn't. We are stuck on milk, as referenced in 1 Corinthians and Hebrews when Paul contrasts "milk" and "meat" in order to make a spiritual analogy. How do we get back to covenant living? How do we learn to dive into an intimate knowledge of God and a calling grounded in what God views as important—not the Reformation, the late church, the world, or anything else . . . simply the Word and life.

I love the idea of really pouring yourself into something. If you are going to do it, then do it right. The Bible refers to this as the heart, mind, and soul. This comes from the Shema in Deuteronomy 6. The biblical authors didn't have a great understanding of how the body or the world worked. God wasn't too concerned about correcting their thoughts either. That wasn't his main directive. He wasn't writing a science or history textbook (although we can learn a lot about science and history through the Bible); he was writing a love story and expressing how people can fully know him and get back to the life and purpose that we were designed to fulfill within his covenant kingdom. One of the most beautiful things about God is that he accepts us where we are but invites us to enter into an amazing, dynamic, growing, and everlasting relationship with him. The ancient authors had no idea how the brain, mind, or the heart worked. They had no concept of what happened where or how, they just knew it happened. We have to, in a way, approach Scripture with the understanding that the authors would have had. It seldom will mean something to us that wasn't intended or understood within the cultural context of the inspired writers. Occasionally prophetic writing can yield itself to a more developed understanding, but for the most part, within Scripture we need to determine what a passage means to us based on the message it had in its original context. For instance, when Deuteronomy speaks of the heart, it is describing the intellect. Today we think of intellect as the mind, but we also realize that it is influenced by the very essence of what gives us life, which is the heart. So, as I speak of the heart, mind, and soul of Deuteronomy 6, there are many words that could describe the author's intended meaning. The Hebrew Bible uses a plethora of words to create this mosaic picture. In our English language and Western culture, these words carry some baggage that they didn't have at the time the Bible was written. For instance, when we think of the word *soul*, we think of a notion that stems from Greek philosophy: a non-physical, immortal presence that dwells inside of us and at death rises from our bodies to find immortality. That is far from what the soul represented in Scripture.

When the Bible talks about the soul of man in the Old Testament, it uses the Hebrew word *nephesh*. Nephesh occurs 700 times in the Bible and is translated with words like *soul, person, being, self, mind, heart, body, appetite, desire* and many others. The New Testament carries the same type of meaning for the word *psuche*. You will notice that all of these words describe life—not death or some kind of afterlife. The biblical authors did have an understanding of what happened after death, but they didn't really associate this word with it. In fact, the biblical authors hardly talked about resurrected life and when they did this isn't the word they used. You don't *have* a *nephesh*; you *are* a nephesh.

*Nephesh* comes from the verb *nâphash*, which is usually translated as "refreshed." A good example is in Exodus 31:17: in six days the LORD made the heavens and the earth, and on the seventh day he rested and was refreshed.»» NIV "In six days the Lᴍ made the heavens and the earth, and on the seventh day he rested and was **refreshed**." One third of all of Old Testament references to *nephesh* refer to the whole of life itself. Another third refer to will, intellect, and emotion, and the rest seem to simply be pronouns describing the actual person or a craving, an appetite, or an ambition.

The Hebrew word for heart is slightly different, yet they are often connected. The words used for heart are *levav* or *lev*. The heart is most often associated with how a person decides or discerns something influenced by desire. Often with heart we also read about strength, the Hebrew word for which is *me'od*. Literally it means "very" or "much." So, when we say we love God with all of our strength, it is actually better interpreted that we are loving him with our everything, literally "muchness," which we just wouldn't say in English. When we get to the New Testament, we see the Greek word *dunamis*, which expresses an idea of power and sometimes wealth, and which is associated with first fruits being offered to God. The idea is that we have the power to give God all that we have been given and the very essence of who we are.

Putting this all together, God made us in his image to bear light (fruit), and dwell in a sacred covenant of life with and in him. He gives us the very gift of life and is honored when we then, in return, give it back. This is the greater calling of Scripture, to give God glory. This held true in the Old Testament and was *really* brought out in the finished work of the cross. We take what we have been given and use it in the kingdom to its full potential as God develops and nurtures it. To love him with all of our heart, mind, and soul means to take every form of what he has given us and return it to him as an investment of multiplication. It means to devote all of yourself as an offering with no limitations to loving God and your neighbor.

When we examine Psalm 16:6, we see a similar Old Testament idea: "The lines have fallen to me in pleasant places, indeed, I have a beautiful inheritance."

The word for inheritance here is *nachalah*. It's one of my favorite Old Testament Hebrew words. At first it appears as if the inheritance is "simply" land. You might get this feeling when you read the same word in Numbers 26:53–56; but there is a bit of fuzziness or mystery enshrouded in it. Notice what seems to be almost a birthright census when describing the inheritance in the chapters preceding this. The emphasis is that it all belongs to the Lord and he desires to reclaim it.

We continue to find this word as we continue through the Old Testament. It doesn't seem to "only" be land, and in fact in many cases land isn't connected to the *nachalah*, but spoken of separately and/or differently. We see this in Deuteronomy 32:8: "When the Most High gave the nations their inheritance, when he divided all mankind, he set up boundaries for the peoples according to the number of the sons of Israel." ("Sons of God" is a better rendering here.)

Verse nine continues the same thought as God talks about them as his treasured possession. Again, like in Numbers 26, there seems to be a spiritual numbering of those who are God's "portion"—another way that this word is used. It signifies a prized position (treasured entity) but is often rendered as if it is a verb performing an action. When the Hebrew language does this in the Bible, it is intentional. We don't have this in English, so a lot of people fail to recognize the significance when things are written this way (and most Americans don't read Hebrew.)

We start to get the idea that the sacred land that God claims is part of the *nachalah* but not the complete *nachalah*. This is very similar to the gospel message that I will expound on later. Many talk about the plan of salvation as if it's the only ingredient of the gospel. As we will see, it is important, but it's not all of the gospel. The gospel itself is more than that, in the same way that *nachalah* is more than simply the Messiah or heaven.

Throughout the pages of the Old Testament, the people of God are asked to simply give all of themselves because they have been God's portion, his treasured possession. Yet we see this phrased in a way that often signifies sacrificial and humble inheritance, which conveys the clear implication that it also means there is more. There is something else.

As if being completely God's isn't enough! But the writers of the Old Testament had no idea what the inheritance was. That is why the proclamation of belonging "of God" is simply to walk in faithful obedience; they had no conception of what the rest of the covenant promise was or might be. It's the childlike faith of the New Testament. We see God telling generations of Old Testament believers that they have inheritance, but it is never completely revealed to them. "Simply follow me in faithfulness and one day the revelation will come and be a gift to everyone regardless of their time on this earth." The inheritance would cover all who had been his. By the time of the kings, the prophets start to pick up on this as a word from God giving hope of redemption; that all that has been lost might be regained as God's possessional people. This message was going to become even greater through the prophets of the exile.

In Psalm 16, David uses the same word to describe the inheritance of the Levites, the priests. But their inheritance was not any part of the land; their inheritance was the Lord himself (Numbers 18:20).

The Levites were given a special relationship with God as the priests of Israel, but this wasn't the "plan A" of the Bible. We see Adam and Eve as the first priests in the Bible until they were expelled from the garden. Plan A was lost. But God continued his covenant by making a new plan to walk (tabernacle) with them. With Israel, that great relationship privilege was most often only granted to the Levites. Every other obedient faithful follower of Yahweh was simply told, "Just wait, the inheritance is also coming to you!" In this sense, the inheritance of the Levites was a special part of a direct relationship with God. It was a foreshadowing of what would later be offered to all through the Messiah.

In Hebraic culture, you didn't have a right to life, liberty, and property (the original wording of the Declaration of Independence). In fact, you didn't have a right to anything. Everything was God's. He made it and controls all things and has the sole right to his creation. Some of these ideas became lost in a mucked-up world, yet God's mission is to still regather and restore the original plan. What started with Eden eschatologically comes to fruition in a picture very much like Eden. When we follow in faithful obedience to him, he gives us life, liberty, and sacred property simply because he is gracious, compassionate, and loving, and more than anything, he desires for you to be completely his.

*Nachalah* is positional (that is why throughout the pages of the text it functions like a verb). For generations the Hebrews walked in simple faith while waiting for the covenant promise of inheritance, despite not having any idea what that meant. In the New Testament the ultimate plan of redemption—to return all believers to priests—is revealed through Jesus coming to the throne at the ascension.

But is that it? I mean that's pretty good right?! We are now recreated sons of God (*bǝnê haĕlōhîm*; note that this is not a gender-specific term as it is in English); in Hebrew this signifies that those directly created by the hand of God and grafted into the kingdom through the cross will be the "ruling priesthood."

We know our inheritance is our position in Christ. We are his and he is in us. Our bodies serve as his temple and our very image represents him; every one of us are divinely marked. Is that it? No!!! Are you ready for this? That isn't all of the inheritance.

> That is why he is the one who mediates a new covenant between God and people, so that all who are called can receive the eternal inheritance God has promised them. For Christ died to set them free from the penalty of the sins they had committed under that first covenant. (Hebrews 9:15 NLT)

In the Old Testament, this is the promised land of Canaan; in the future it is the recreated heavens and earth. Is the inheritance that we will rule? Yes, that's part of it; we find that in many places in the New Testament, such as 1 Corinthians 6:3. But read carefully. The grammar signifies that although the land, the ruling, and the grafting as sons of God are all described as inheritance, there is still more. This just keeps getting better and better . . . (by the way, that in itself communicates the character of God!)

In New Testament Greek, the same word is rendered as *klerononeo*, which simply means "to be an heir to." The flavor by which it is described takes on an idea of "to receive as one's own, to obtain, or to possess oneself of." This means that "inheriting" is provided through and in Christ; and all that is contained in that hope is grounded on the promises of God.

The New Testament seems to continually imply that there is more. That we know of some of the inheritance—our position in Christ, the eschatological sacred land, the gifting given—but there is still an element of something else. A mystery. What is it? I don't know.

But I know there is something more, and it seems like we were intentionally not told what it might be. When they didn't know the Messiah was coming in the Old Testament, they just knew to walk in faith; in the same way, in the New Testament we are also not told of the complete inheritance but still told to simply walk in faith. In Hebrew, all things are circular. This "dance of grace" given and received is to be taken and in the same way re-given out again.

I don't know my complete inheritance. I'm not dwelling on it as some great reward. It's never been about pie-in-the-sky thinking. We walk because the relational journey is life itself and part of what it means to bear the image of the Creator.

Today I ask you to consider what God has given you and how you can fully give it back in sacred devotion to him. Ask someone in your spiritual family to identify what God has given you and assess how you have used this and can continue to use all of the recipe of who God has made you to be in him. I encourage you to vision-cast. What does success in God's eyes look like for your life. Often, we want to size success up by the world's standards and not by God's. Change your way of thinking. Let Scripture determine value and worth. The kingdom of God way of thinking is very different than the kingdom of the world. In many ways it is opposite or upside-down that is really right-side-up. The first shall be last, turn the other cheek, the king on a cross. Don't let your covenant-sacred standards be influenced by worldly thinking. What does God say is important for your life? Too often we don't strategize what godly eternal life looks like.

We have personal investment strategies, work goals, visions for retirement and everything else, but we seldom stop to evaluate what means more than all those things. Think Yahweh, think complete giving of the heart, mind, and soul; think big, *nephesh* living.

*YouTube Expedition44 keyword search: Soul*

CHAPTER 4

# Covenant Kingdom Living | Genesis 2–3 and Revelation 21– 22

"Our relationship with God is not contractual, so that we could fulfill the right conditions and it would have the desired results, as if our relationship with God resembled putting coins in a vending machine. It is a personal relationship, and such relationships involve freedom on both sides."

John E. Goldingay, *Do We Need the New Testament?: Letting the Old Testament Speak for Itself*

There is a common notion today that since we live under a new covenant that began with Jesus, the Old Testament way of thinking and living has been completely abolished. I alluded to this in the previous chapter. We think that way because Jesus clearly established a new covenant or promise for those who follow him, which taught that you no longer necessarily have to follow the Old Testament law.

To fully understand the new covenant you have to first understand the previous covenants. A covenant is simply a promise between two parties. When someone speaks of covenant living, they usually mean our relationship with God. There are five major covenants in the Bible. Some are conditional, meaning God says if you do this, then I will do that for you. Others are non-conditional, meaning God is just offering a covenant to you. Those are still conditional in many ways: even though they are offered to us with no real conditions, we still need to accept them. These covenants are the Noahic covenant, the Abrahamic covenant, the Mosaic covenant, the Davidic covenant, and the new covenant.

Out of these covenants, we all know that today we are under the new covenant, which was established by Jesus's life, culminated on the cross, and decreed through the ascension. There is a feeling within the New Testament that we don't necessarily need to follow the Mosaic covenant anymore, as it was given to keep God's chosen people (Israel) on course until the Messiah came. The law was established as a stopgap to show how to follow Yahweh until the written word of God and God himself in the form of man (Jesus) could come to us and set the record straight. The conundrum of following Jesus is that Jesus both followed the law perfectly and said to "do as I do" or "follow me." Now some might argue that Jesus healed on the Sabbath and so he didn't fully follow the law. Most will agree that he did fully follow the Mosaic law though, just not the rabbinical law of the Jews. Does this mean you and I should actually follow the Mosaic law? Well, no: Paul clearly teaches that following every part of the Mosaic law is no longer necessary and in fact today wouldn't really be possible. In actuality, it was never fully possible, even for Israel.

The law could never be fully followed. No person until Jesus was ever successful in following all of the law. Today we have the same problem under the new covenant. God created the world and everything in it as "good." Notice he didn't say perfect. Have you ever considered why?

God starts things in the garden of Eden by establishing the way he wants to walk and live with his creation, humankind. He creates a good world and then asks man and woman to help him continue to cultivate and watch over and work this creation in a partnership with him. This is essentially the life he created us for. So, whether you believe Adam and Eve were the first people or not (this is a deeper biblical argument than you might realize), we can agree that Genesis 1 and 2 present Adam and Eve as having both a kingly role and a priestly role; they are the first God-established king-priests in the Bible. The important thing here is that God started the world the way he wanted it. He established a relationship or covenant with humankind so that through the choices that we make by our free will, we give ultimate glory to God by accepting and entering into covenant living.

Now we all know that this did not last long in the garden. The Satan/serpent figure entered the story, and, because of man's ability to freely choose, even the established king-priests stepped outside of their relationship with God. From that point on, the narrative begins a reoccurring circular rejection of God resulting in a downward spiral for mankind. We can't possibly find our way back to the garden . . . or can we? God chose to give us another chance, a chance that one eternal day will allow us to return to the way of life he designed for us—a new Eden, life eternal. Heaven is where we go to be with Christ on the throne when we die. We all know that, right? But what you might not realize is that, similar to paradise in the Old Testament, heaven is not our final destination. Our final destination is a new, recreated heaven on earth: a new Eden established for God's kingdom, forever ruling with him in a great partnership covenant as kings and priests.

The Bible gives us a few clues about this. Paul says in Philippians 1:21–23 **21**For to me, to live is Christ and to die is gain. **22**If I am to go on living in the body, this will mean fruitful labor for me. Yet what shall I choose? I do not know! **23**I am torn between the two: I desire to depart and be with Christ, which is better by far;." At the final resurrection, it seems we may get a physical body back.

When "the times reach their fulfillment," God will "bring unity to all things in heaven and on earth under Christ" (Ephesians 1:10).

Today I want you to consider something deeper. At some point in both the Old and New Testaments, God gives us things. He tells us how we can enter into this great covenant with him and how we can best give him glory. In the Old Testament, some things were given (like the law) as a stopgap to combat a fallen world with fallen entities; to keep us on track with God's holy plan. But some things are given because they are God's ideal way of relationship with us. When God first went into a covenant with Israel, he established a direct "rule" by him. This was called a theocracy. Eventually people asked for a king, and, surprisingly, God gave one to them, even though it wasn't his way. Sadly, his kingdom repeatedly chose a different path throughout biblical history. Today I urge you to consider God's primary offering, a covenant based on his ways, not mankind's ways. The Bible doesn't actually tell us what all of these "ideals" might be. Are we being given the ideal directive from God or is God simply meeting us as a steppingstone? Why doesn't the Bible simply have a list of ways to ideally follow? The answer is in the heart. God's heart in this offering is to walk with us and be honored by our choosing his way of thinking, and for his way of living to be given back to him by the same heart offering.

Continuing our thoughts from Chapter 3: do your time, money, and talent signify that God is your first priority? Does everyone around you know that your primary directive is to faithfully live a life and calling for the kingdom of God? What are you doing well, and what can you do better? Jesus is on the throne since he ascended and he is asking us to fully and unequivocally live for him now as a living sacrifice, making our body and our life itself (*nephesh*) a sacred temple to bear his light within us as a living covenant offering. He is our king. We are living in his kingdom right now and have the hope that we will one day walk with him in the new heaven on earth, just as we did in Eden.

*YouTube Expedition44 keyword search: Covenant discipleship, heaven*

# CHAPTER 5

# The Image of God | Deuteronomy 26 and Exodus 3

The law envisions a different kind of life, characterized by self-discipline and self-giving love. Imagine a community where every member actively worked to love and protect their neighbor!

—Carmen Joy Imes, *Bearing God's Name: Why Sinai Still Matters*

Today the average American gets up every Monday morning, goes to work for 8–9 hours a day, and probably either works another 5–6 hours on Saturday to pick up some overtime or has some kind of a side hustle. We essentially have bought into the American way of thinking that the most important things in life are material assets. Materialism has trumped things that truly matter. We spend the greater part of our time and energy working, and then give what we have left back to the things that should rank much higher. From a biblical perspective this is the biggest problem with the great American way of life. We have chosen to (practically) worship the material mindset because everyone else has sold out to that way of thinking. Take a step back for a moment and consider the cost. It really is nearly impossible to live a fully committed life as a Christian with this American problem. As followers of Christ, we are called to put him first. When we choose to work fifty hours a week and give the best energy of your life to that endeavor, how can we possibly be thinking about putting God first? Quite frankly, are a nice home, new cars, and vacations once or twice a year really better? How do Christians let themselves get buried in such material thinking? Didn't Jesus tell us point blank not to put anything else in front of him?

In the Old Testament, God told his people that he wanted their best first. It wasn't simply money, like we think of a tithe or offering in church today; it was much more. He wanted their hearts. He gave us everything, and in turn is honored when, out of the free will of our hearts, we essentially offer all he has given us back to him. It's reciprocal giving out of a desire to give intimately of all you have and are. In the Old Testament, one person's life essentially existed as a part of a whole community that honored God with its way of life. In the New Testament, Christ continued and perfected that way of thinking.

"First fruits" refers to the first portion of the harvest, which was given back to God. This was more than a gift; it was a way of life. You made a pledge before God that the best of not only what you had, but of who you were would be offered back to the Lord as a living sacrifice. Israel was reminded of this way of living every year in ritual celebrations such as the feasts. Today it sounds strange to us that nearly half of the Israelites' lives were spent wining and dining in feasts . . . in fact they didn't even really "work" like we think of work. We really have no concept or understanding of this way of life, so it seems foreign to most.

All of these reflections of first fruits (the Feast of Weeks [Shavuot] in Numbers 28:26; Tabernacles [Sukkot] in Exodus 23:16; and Passover in Leviticus 23:10) reflect a greater plan that God had for his people. Later we see this kind of thinking come to fruition when Christ in his resurrection is called "the first fruits of those who have fallen asleep" (1 Corinthians 15:20–23). There are many connections that I get into on video on the Expedition44 YouTube channel, but as a foundation, it is important to simply understand that Jesus gave his life as our Passover lamb & rose as the first to be resurrected, but all who trust in him will also rise from the dead in the final "harvest." Jesus is the first of the recreated sons of God grafted into the new covenant.

## Bearing the Image of God by Covenant Living

The entire biblical narrative is the story of how our relationship means so much to God that he created an extravagant plan to regain what was lost in the fall and return his treasured creation to a sacred relationship with him. As we learned in the last chapter, the endgame looks a lot like the picture we started with in Eden, a recreated sacred heaven and earth where God rules with his created beings.

Why do you exist within this relational dynamic kingdom? Where are you in the pages of this story?

"So the LORD God took the man [he had made] and settled him in the Garden of Eden to cultivate and keep it" (Genesis 2:15, Amplified Bible). Adam and Eve were created and set apart to function in relationship with God in a role or vocation that the Bible describes as keepers and cultivators. The word *cultivate* is the Hebrew word abad, which is the calling to serve. *Keep* is the Hebrew word *shamar*, meaning to guard. These ideas are also reiterated as the same two verbs given together when Moses explains the duties of the Levitical priests (Numbers 3:6–8; 3:31, 36; 4:28; 8:25–26; 18:1–7).

Every being that God created had a specific function, position, or role. The angels were messengers; the cherubim were the spiritual beings that functioned as guards (part of our vocational calling was immediately passed on to them); the seraphim (Isaiah 6) offered purification through their lips (we like to call this singing but it has far deeper spiritual implications).

Remember the snake in the garden? Some translations say "serpent"; others read "snake"; in Hebrew the word is *nachash*. The word *nachash* in Scripture and other ancient writings takes on the ability of healing. Today it still carries this connotation. The international symbol of medicine, the herald's staff, depicts a snake on a pole.

John 3 says, "And as Moses lifted up the serpent in the wilderness, so must the Son of Man be lifted up, that whoever believes in him may have eternal life." Spiritual healing through the atonement of Christ is compared to the healing given through the snake "lifted up" in the wilderness.

The serpent was likely in the garden to perform a positive function—to heal. But upon his rebellion he took what was good from God and turned it to sin. Throughout the rest of the Old Testament the Hebrew word for "sorcery" or "witchcraft" is the same as the word for serpent. We have a created being that had a spiritual role in the garden to do good, but willfully chose the opposite and in doing so deceived Adam and Eve to also give up their God-given roles. The *nachash*, the deceiver, makes a choice to fall, bringing God's prized relational entities down with him.

At the core of this cosmic struggle, what exactly is it that the deceiver is doing? He is trying to remove the God-given vocation of God's prized beings. Since the very beginning, Satan has sought to destroy our intended role in our relationship with God: to walk in covenant with him and bear his light in the darkness.

Genesis 1:26–27 says that God made humankind in his "image" and "likeness." The meaning of "in" is function. In Hebrew this word acts more like a verb than noun (this is fairly common in the Hebrew language). When we place obedient faith in (Hebrew tissa—to bear; to carry; to support; to lift) him, we become recreated sons of God. The term carries no implied gender in Hebrew. All of humankind are called sons of God. That's why some like to translate this in English as "sons and daughters of God."

In ancient times kings would erect monuments throughout their kingdoms to clearly define the boundaries of their land and define ownership. The images of the king communicated who the people were to serve or live in allegiance to. There were also images of the gods. These weren't intended to be the god's themselves, but represented a god whose place was likely in a temple or heavenly domain. These images were reminders of the authorities that people lived in and under.

Humankind has been given the authority to rule over the other creatures God has made; *we have that authority because humankind is made in God's image.* "You shall have no other gods before me.(Exodus 20:3 NIV), and "Don't worship any images whatsoever" (Exodus 20:4–6 NIV). In all the other civilizations, people simply lived under the king and the spiritual beings. God created us in his image that we might be both grafted in the heritage of the kingdom as royalty but also spiritually as priests. That is why when we read Psalm 8:4–6 we find the amazingly high description of the life and calling of humankind:

> What is man that You take thought of him,
> And the son of man that You care for him?
> Yet You have made him a little lower than God,
> And You crown him with glory and majesty!
> You make him to rule over the works of Your hands;
> You have put all things under his feet,
> All sheep and oxen,
> And also the beasts of the field,
> The birds of the heavens and the fish of the sea,
> Whatever passes through the paths of the seas.
> O LORD, our Lord,
> How majestic is Your name in all the earth!

In its original context, this passage describes us, humanity. It also has a dual Hebraic meaning as it also serves as a foreshadowing of the Messiah. In Exodus 3 God appears to Moses:

> But Moses said to God, "Who am I, that I should go to Pharaoh, and that I should bring the sons of Israel out of Egypt?" And He said, "Certainly I will be with you, and this shall be the sign to you that it is I who have sent you: when you have

brought the people out of Egypt, you shall worship God at this mountain."Moses's reply to God seems humble, like that of a lowly shepherd servant. God's reply is fitting: a simple yet powerful response saying, "I will be with you." Moses was royalty in Egypt, yet he was still in spiritual bondage. God freed him, yet Moses spent the next forty years in the wilderness. In the Old Testament, the wilderness is symbolic for depression, trials, and training. I am sure Moses was questioning God.

Sometimes we don't know when we are in training, when God is preparing us for something bigger. God simply asks us to faithfully follow as we bear his name.

In Scripture, we often find examples of faithfulness in small kingdom-related tasks being rewarded with larger ones. This is the calling of a backwards kingdom, where the lowly shepherds who should be last are first. It is also important to realize that this isn't about our material skill, possession, or ability. The predominant message here is that God is enough, he is our all. "I will be with you."

When I pray for my kids, that's all I pray for. There is nothing else. Every parent wants their kids to flourish, but let's think of success with kingdom eyes. As long as God is "with them," that's all I care about.

I have a good friend. By the world's standards he doesn't amount to much. He drives cars that are given to him, he has never had a real job, and he certainly doesn't have any kind of retirement account. Every day his sole purpose is to simply be Jesus to others. He hangs out at grocery stores and helps people load groceries, he posts "Free Help" ads on bulletin boards, he is at every football game on the corner with a cross. But this is my favorite: he sits on the side of the road on mornings with a sign that reads "Free prayer," and he has a line every day. This is a king of a great kingdom.

When Moses finally accepts God's calling, he is commissioned. God will be in him and asks Moses that he commission the nation of Israel in the same way. Exodus 19 reads:

> On the first day of the third month after the Israelites left Egypt—on that very day—they came to the Desert of Sinai. After they set out from Rephidim, they entered the Desert of Sinai, and Israel camped there in the desert in front of the mountain.
>
> Then Moses went up to God, and the LORD called to him from the mountain and said, "This is what you are to say

to the descendants of Jacob and what you are
to tell the people of Israel: 'You yourselves have
seen what I did to Egypt, and how I carried you
on eagles' wings and brought you to myself. Now
if you obey me fully and keep my covenant, then
out of all nations you will be my treasured possession. Although the whole earth is mine, you[a] will
be for me a kingdom of priests and a holy nation.' These are the words you are to speak to the
Israelites."

Some translations interpret this as a "treasured possession"; others call it "his portion." This is another dual Hebraic meaning—it
takes on the meaning of both. You might prefer the term "portion" from the earlier chapters or if you are aware of a Deuteronomy 32 worldview. It does mean that, but also means treasured
possession (*segullah*). This is more clear in the ESV version of
Psalm 135:4: "For the L⃞ has chosen Jacob for himself, Israel as
his own possession [*segullah*]."

What God is asking Moses to charge Israel with is simple. They
would be his *chosen portion, his beloved people, holy and set apart as his
treasured possession.* God wants them to represent Yahweh among the
nations, to obey God fully and keep his covenant, and give their exclu-
sive loyalty and allegiance to him. This comes to fruition in his commandments when he says, "Thou shalt not take the name of the Lord
thy God in vain." He is asking that his people, created in his very image,
represent God to the world as a priestly calling. The thrust of the message is that they do not misrepresent his name or image in vain.

Let's retrace. Adam and Eve were created to keep and cultivate but
fell. The plan for Abraham's descendants in covenant was to reach all
nations. I wouldn't say that plan failed but it was modified in the calling of Israel after the cosmic disarray of the tower of Babel, when God
seemingly changed gears to work through Israel as his portion. Unfor-

tunately, Israel failed God as well and was eventually given over to judgment and exile. However, in God's continued faithfulness to regain his plan for us to rule with him, he sent his Son to reconcile everything as the seed of Israel.

1 Peter 2:9 (NIV) says, "But you are a chosen people, a royal priesthood, a holy nation, God's special possession, that you may declare the praises of him who called you out of darkness into his wonderful light." Peter takes the status of Israel and applies it to the whole church. You and I are grafted into this calling as recreated sons of God in the royal priestly calling. We become God's portion, his treasured possession, the royal priesthood with the vocation to solely bear the image of God and be a representation of him to the nations, bringing the people to God and God to the people. We are literally the exact representation and being of the King. Christ lives in us as our bodies are sacred, set-apart temples of the Lord.

In Hebrews 2:5–9, the anonymous author cites Psalm 8. What he is doing is framing Jesus as the "*firstborn* over all creation" (v. 15). As *firstborn* over creation, Jesus, in his resurrection, "completes" the calling of us to be able to return to the intended status that God created us for. Jesus is the full image-bearer of God and functions as the restorative Savior of humanity to regain the priestly and royal lineage as sons of God.

Paul says in Philippians 2:6–7 that "Jesus humbled himself" (v. 8). From the beginning this has been our calling. To humbly serve. Being part of the renewed image of God means being "conformed to the image" of Jesus (Romans 8:29). The journey is to become exceedingly more like Christ, to bear his very image.

There is also a more eschatological understanding of our position in Christ as a ruling authority. 2 Timothy 2:12 (NASB) says, "If we endure, we shall also reign with him." And 1 Corinthians 6:2–3 asks, "Do you not know that the saints will judge the world? (NASB) And if the world will be judged by you, are you unworthy to judge the smallest matters? Do you not know that we shall judge angels? How much more things that pertain to this life?"

I don't know what this means exactly. As I often say, we don't get the whole picture or story. We just get what is given and that is the mystery of the gospel. It seems that the final step of the Christian journey is becoming the eschatological ruling authority with God. We return to an Eden-like setting where we keep and cultivate.

To sum up the concept of bearing the image of God, there is an underlying covenant commitment to giving your life to follow God as you are called in your royal priesthood. If this is exactly what you were designed to do, your primary directive in life, then how are you doing? Are you the picture of a successful kingdom priest? The mindset of obedience seems very different than what we have been seasoned to think in our modern culture. When we say "I gave my life to Jesus," it carries a connotation of momentary salvation. Yet God is the only one that can judge the heart. I would challenge people to look at belief or following Jesus as less of a momentary experience and more of a lifelong journey. Scripturally, the idea of "belief in God" had a different understanding in the Old Testament than it does today. It meant that you were obedient and allegiant to bear the name of God, holy and set apart, with a complete calling to represent the exact image and name of God to the nations. We are aliens living in a foreign land and our "citizenship is in heaven."

I come back to the question, where are you in this story? Many of us are entangled in the world. In some of his last words to Timothy, Paul wrote that "no soldier in active service entangles himself in the affairs of everyday life ["civilian pursuits"], so that he may please the One Who enlisted him as a soldier" (2 Timothy 2:4 NASB). Many of us are way too entangled in this world. As I said at the beginning of this chapter, the way we live in our culture seems so far from what the biblical mosaic of living as a royal priesthood embodies. Do your time, treasure, and talent reflect whom God has called you to be? Is your vocation to show the image of God, lighting the way in a dark and murky world?

When my oldest son was very young, we would wake up every Thursday at 5:30 a.m. for a grand event. The garbage man. I don't know what it is about a garbage truck when you are five years old, but it was amazing! He was mesmerized by the idea of being a garbage man. My wife and I have come to realize that we don't really care what our children do in life from the world's perspective. We just pray that they may have a heart to invite God to fully live in them.

Maybe today you are trying really hard to be someone that you weren't designed to be. Maybe you never knew that your worth was not in your image but completely in God's. Maybe you're valuing your impact, your legacy, on what the world says matters. Perhaps it is time to re-evaluate from God's eyes. 1 Samuel 17:45–47 is awesome: it describes a young boy who finds a nation cowering and boldly represents God to the nations. Upon defeating the giant, he says, "So that all the earth may know that there is a God in Israel." (NASB) May we represent God in such a way that the whole earth may know.

---

Today I encourage you to consider a more "priestly" way of living. Do you really need the bling of American life? Doesn't it make more since to give God your best? Your best time of the day, your best talent, and what you hold most important, your spouse and family. What if you didn't buy into this American dream? What if it were possible to spend your time and invest in things of greater eternal value. Love God and love your neighbor. It's not that I don't believe in work. God gave us work as part of his ideal life for us in the garden. But it was kingdom work; after man fell, the mindset of work started changing from joy to toil, which is where most Americans are today. Return to godly living and kingdom work and eternal thinking. Receive your royal priestly calling.

---

*YouTube Expedition44 keyword search: Covenant, first fruits, image bearing, light*

CHAPTER 6

# Who Is Your King? |
# Deuteronomy 6

I believe a significant segment of American evangelicalism is guilty of nationalistic and political idolatry. To a frightful degree, I think, evangelicals fuse the kingdom of God with a preferred version of the kingdom of the world (whether it's our national interests, a particular form of government, a particular political program, or so on). Rather than focusing our understanding of God's kingdom on the person of Jesus—who, incidentally, never allowed himself to get pulled into the political disputes of his day—I believe many of us American evangelicals have allowed our understanding of the kingdom of God to be polluted with political ideals, agendas, and issues.

Gregory A. Boyd, *The Myth of a Christian Nation: How the Quest for Political Power Is Destroying the Church*

Today when we talk about kings we are immediately taken back to ancient thinking. It makes sense in many ways; within recent history kings have simply become showpieces for countries rather than the sovereign authority of a land. In America, the idea of a royal king has for the most part been replaced by political parties. Particularly during the Trump presidency, many Christians seemed to equate voting Republican as voting Christian . . . but trust me, I don't want to get into politics! Quite the opposite, in fact. I would, however, ask you to consider your allegiances.

At some point, we have all considered ourselves a citizen of the kingdom of God. We say all the time that we are aliens living in a foreign land and that our "citizenship is in heaven." I bet you have said this before, but do you actually believe it and live for it? The last chapter set a foundation for thinking this way, countercultural to the world.

In the Old Testament, God established a direct rule (theocracy) under himself, "the one true God." Why do you think he describes himself this way? This may surprise you, but there were other gods in the Old Testament. They weren't just made-up facets of people's imagination or simply idols, although they were represented by idols. They were likely fallen spiritual beings such as the serpent figure. Revelation tells us that eventually one-third of all the spiritual beings will fall. At the cross Jesus bound these entities. They likely no longer "rule" like they once did. But in the Old Testament, when you confessed a belief in Yahweh, you were asserting allegiance to the one true God over the many others. God called his people to this kind of allegiance throughout the Old Testament. When we read in the New Testament that you can't serve two masters (Matthew 6), this is how they would have understood it. Paul tells Timothy not to be caught up in "civilian affairs." Sounds like Paul is in the army and his obedience should only be to his king, no one else. As we live in the world but not of the world, we start to be reminded of this kind of allegiance. This is truly what it means to seek first the kingdom of God . . . and there is no second. All of you and everything you have; a complete *nephesh* way of living.

I often hear people raising up America so radically, especially during times of presidential elections. I see people with flags in their yards, stickers on their trucks, internet conversations, and so much more, proclaiming how patriotic they are. I see discussions about what president a Christian should vote for, or if a person's policy on a Christian issue solely warrants a vote.

In the Bible, God takes on many titles such as Lord, Christ, and Messiah. These titles represent the supreme authority in your life. In other words, if you're claiming these titles, then there can be no one else. The Bible addresses people's allegiance to the kingdoms and empires of the world in many ways.

Consider this. America has a constitution that we all affirm, and we have those we hold up as heroes whom we nearly worship as well. Remember the Lincoln Memorial? Did you know that it nearly exactly represents a Greek temple? Have you ever read what is written behind Lincoln?

> IN THIS TEMPLE
> AS IN THE HEARTS OF THE PEOPLE
> FOR WHOM HE SAVED THE UNION
> THE MEMORY OF ABRAHAM LINCOLN
> S ENSHRINED FOREVER

We have days that the entire nation observes; we even have hymns! Now don't get me wrong here: some of my best friends are veterans and we are indebted to their service. But often we hold this patriotism too high as Christians. You may not have realized it before now, but consider everything I've mentioned. We have sacred texts, saints, temples or sacred ground, and holy days; it sounds as if American nationalism has become a religion.

Traditional Jews grow up reciting a section of Deuteronomy called the Shema. It is essentially a daily devotion to get their mind focused on honoring God with all that they are (heart, mind, and soul). It is recited at the beginning of every day and reiterated throughout the day. This might catch you a little off guard, but we have been trained from a young age to do this in America as well. It's called the Pledge of Allegiance. Every morning our sons and daughters in their schools give allegiance to our country. Doesn't really seem wrong until you ask the question, "Shouldn't that kind of allegiance be to God alone?"

Lastly, many Christians, if not all of them, close their prayers with the word *amen*. We typically understand this word to mean "so be it," which in our American thinking doesn't really make a lot of sense. In Hebrew, the root means "to be faithful," which was a regular declaration of your complete obedience. In the Hebrew mindset, the day starts off with the Shema and is reaffirmed after each prayer throughout the day with the same allegiance.

I want to challenge you here. The way that people have gravitated toward worshipping their country over God didn't just happen all at once. It took them over slowly. This is an addiction.

Addiction is one of the nastiest spiritual strongholds of the world.

> For even though they knew God, they did not honor him as God or give thanks, but they became futile in their speculations, and their foolish heart was darkened. (Romans 1:21 NASB)

Usually when we think of addictions, we frame the idea in our minds as drug abuse. But there are a lot of other addictions of the mind, and they can be destructive with deep and far-reaching (generational) spiritual and worldly consequences.

The way God designed your mind to work, innately and wonderfully designed from the beginning, is for you to have the ability to condition and train it. It's a beautiful thing, but it's also a scary thing. Every time you make a decision you are conditioning your mind one way or another. When we make great (kingdom principle) decisions, we are conditioning our minds to lean toward God; when we make poor (worldly) decisions we are conditioning our minds to be entrenched in what becomes an automatic way of coping and giving into the desires of the world. Eventually this leads to an addiction to those things.

Most read this passage from Paul (Romans 1:21 above) from the perspective that he's just talking to those who are not with Christ. This is one of my pet peeves: we often read everything as simply salvific. Our Western culture has conditioned us this way. I challenge you to take this Scripture and, even though it's talking about those in darkness, learn from these principles as they apply to your life.

This passage outlines two really important things: God and gratefulness. How do we recover when our mind has been negatively altered? It's more than just a profession of the mouth, it's an acknowledgment and an action of giving back to God that which is his: our complete self and mind.

Scripture says over and over that God wants our hearts and our minds. That's why he instructed his people in the law to pray for these two things three times a day. Every time we lose the war of cognitive decision-making, we are denying the sovereignty of God, essentially saying that we're not giving him control in our lives.

There is another element to this—being grateful. When we're not grateful, it alters our hearts. And again, what God wants more than anything is to have our complete hearts. When we're ungrateful, we're telling God that we're not claiming our true identity in him. When we continue to be ungrateful over and over, it can lead to addictive behavior. In the Old Testament the wrath of God is shown when God takes his hand away from someone or a group of people and gives them over to something. (In Hebrew it says "his nose becomes long"—I'll leave that puzzle for you to ponder today!) God's wrath is simply a result of ungratefulness that results in broken divine covenant with him.

The good news is that in the same way we have repeatedly made decisions that take us to addiction, we can also make decisions that lead to restoration with God. And an even better part of this is that sometimes, through God's amazing power in us, this transformation can happen immediately—or at least much quicker than the road that we took to degradation.

Gratefulness turns our world into a journey toward God, no matter the stage of our soul or heart. When God draws us out of the disaster that we created, we become grateful again and are filled with joy. Contextually, when we read Paul simply talking to the unsaved, we miss all of this. In our American thinking we dismiss these principles as if they weren't meant for us. This is the disease of American salvific thinking, and I'm convinced that it is one of Satan's (evil "principalities and powers" in Paul's words) greatest tools in derailing the life of a Christian.

But then the question is, how do you recover when you find that your vessel has gone astray? It's by rediscovering positive decision-making over and over again that we're pointed back up toward the people we were designed to be . . . image bearers.

It's taking strategic stands and actions to be set apart in developing a new mind and a new heart.

But isn't that the goal for everyone—not just the addicted, or those that recognize their addictions? As you read this, my challenge to you is to be strategic about making positive, godly kingdom choices in your life with every decision, each and every day, that your heart might be conditioned to bear light and not darkness.

If we are created to be light bearers of the one true God and follow Jesus with everything we are, shouldn't even our political allegiance be clearly for God, not our country or land? Have you become an addict to nationalism? Consider making positive decisions to take back a heart of God. Decisions of God's kingdom, not man's; of God's way of living, not man's. Unfortunately, as much as I love the freedom in our country, nationalism has become an idol or even an addiction to many today. Maybe I should ask you, whose flag are you flying? Ever see a church fly an American flag "over" or instead of a Christian flag? What would Jesus think or say about that flag in the front of the temple?

Whom do you follow? Whom do you live for? What king do you serve? What do your time, treasures, and talents say is the "lord" of your life? Do you "live" in the kingdom of light or the kingdom of this world? Whom is your allegiance to? Honor your king with all that you are. Live in the land but understand that your kingdom is not of this world. And lastly, stop giving any of your heart, mind, and soul to anything that isn't within God's calling for your life. Don't let your heart become addicted to the ways of the world. We only have one king, and that is King Jesus.

*YouTube Expedition44 keyword search: Politics & Deuteronomy 32*

# CHAPTER 7

# The Gospel According to Whom? | Matthew, Mark, Luke, and John

The gospel is the power-releasing story of how Jesus became king and the only adequate response is allegiance alone.

Human salvation is directed toward God's intention to restore individuals, communities, and the world as the kingdom of God continues to break into history. When we give allegiance [to the Lord Jesus Christ], we become new creatures set free from the enslaving power of sin. As we worship the Son of God, who is the authentic, original image of God, our own distorted Adamic image is transformed, so that we are personally renewed. As we are transformed into the image of Jesus the Christ, we bring God's wise service, stewardship, and rule to one another and to the remainder of creation.

Matthew W. Bates, *Salvation by Allegiance Alone: Rethinking Faith, Works, and the Gospel of Jesus the King*

It seems that the church as a whole is confused about what we are supposed to be doing or accomplishing as Christ's followers. Let's just say that you were trapped in a bubble your entire life and had never heard of or read the Bible before. Then, when you came out of your bubble, I handed you a Bible. I told you that it was going to change your life. In fact, I told you that it in and of itself was essentially the very meaning of life. I think I would have your attention; you would probably read it cover to cover in less than a week and it would completely change your life. (As a sidenote, likely no one would do this today; that is part of my point throughout this book. We don't have this priority in life today. But if you had just come out of a bubble and were handed a book with the meaning of life in it, you would read it vigorously.) Had you been in a bubble and then read this book, what do you think your perspective of the Bible would be? How would you see the message or interpret exactly what to do with the new knowldege you had been given? We have all been given the book, yet the message has somehow become very distorted or perhaps distracted. Perhaps this is the greatest accomplishment of the enemy.

There are a few things that I think we have gotten far away from that are central to the gospel. I could name several of these—starting with the church being very different from what I read in Acts—but the main issue that seems to encapsulate everything is the primary directive. The message, the good news, or, as many call it, the gospel. Take three pastors from three different churches from the same town and put them into a room and ask them what the gospel is and you're likely to get three very different answers. How can the message be so vague when it seems to be the primary mission of not just Jesus but the entire Word of God?

First let me describe what the gospel is not. Many have learned a cute little way to tell the story of the Bible and lead people to be momentarily convinced of Jesus, to put all their eggs in a basket to avoid eternal torment and get to the pearly gates; to repent, accept, believe, and be saved. There are many versions of this but the one we may be most familiar with is the Romans Road or some kind of step-by-step system to salvation, as if this is some kind of biblical formula. There are several problems with this kind of thinking but the primary problem is that it doesn't seem to be found in the core of the message when read together as a whole—or, quite frankly, anywhere in the pages of Scripture. There is no step-by-step chart in the Bible. If that was the intention of God himself in his Word, don't you think a simple chart would have been included?

So then, what is the gospel? This is pretty basic to Christianity, yet we have made it out to be so confusing. If we can't answer this as Christians then what are we doing? *Many of us understand only part of the gospel, or understand part of the gospel to be the complete gospel.* The Bible literally calls the gospel the "good news"; the word for that is *euengelion*. If you have never done a simple word study in the Greek, it is worth the investment to start here. This word is introduced at the announcement of Christ's birth and carries forward to become our calling as Christians. The word originally signifies the idea of good tidings, but as we work our way through Scripture (ironically, in what we refer to as "the Gospels" or the books that tell the story of Jesus), we find that the word begins to take on a similar yet different meaning. Take for instance a passage like Mark 1:14–15: "The time has been fulfilled, and the kingdom of God has drawn near; repent and believe in the gospel." (NASB) Has the meaning of the word changed, stayed the same, or taken on a broader meaning?

What about Luke 4:18–19: "The Spirit of the Lord is upon me, because he has anointed me to proclaim good news to the poor. He has sent me to proclaim release to the captives and the regaining of sight to the blind, to set free those who are oppressed, to proclaim the year of the Lord's favor." (NASB)

The answer is in the covenants and the context of the entire lens of the Bible. When I say you can't clearly understand the message of the Bible without understanding covenant thinking, this is what I mean. Many have failed to see the gospel in the Old Testament, and that is problematic to understanding the complete message of the gospel. In Galatians 3:8 we read that God made a covenant with Abraham. We usually call the this the Abrahamic covenant, but it is actually more clearly called the covenant of circumcision. Essentially the message from God to Abraham was that all nations would be blessed through his lineage. (In the next chapter we are going to walk through this story, but for now let's simply leave it that.) Many generations went by, and all failed to live intimately with God. We see the fall in the garden, the flood, the Tower of Babel, and God taking on Israel as his chosen people (or portion of all the world). Eventually they fail him too, and he allows them to go into exile and judgment. But he doesn't lose everyone throughout those years. Some remain faithful and some turn back to him. The faithful are called the remnant. The Old Testament closes with an idea that the Messiah will come to not only deliver the faithful remnant but possibly even the rest as well. Those that have fallen short (all of us in some way) and lost their allegiance will be given a chance to find their way back into this covenant of intimacy with God; to be "adopted" into the kingdom. But as we read, we also find that even the remnant is blemished and (despite ritual yearly cleansing through faithful sacrifice) still will not "make the cut." So not only is the good news for the unfaithful to return to faithfulness, but even for the faithful to now be made complete. The good news is for everyone. And this is essentially the gospel in a simple nutshell.

This plan by original design would be the greatest message to the earth; it would be the "good news" that the world needed to receive after the realization that it had lost, or given up, its right to the kingdom by refusing God.

To the Jews, God's chosen people, it meant a return from exile. To the gentiles, it meant a reclaiming of all people by God by the covenant of Abraham. To the spiritual beings, it meant that the fallen would be bound and a promise or covenant that ensured victory had been won. To all, it meant a return of the original plan to be in intimate relationship and walk with God in a covenant vocation with him. We are all light bearers who will eventually inherit a new kingdom merged with the heavenly realms and a sacred space on the earth.

We have been given the opportunity to be with God in intimate sacred living once again and all we have to do is, by our free will, accept the new covenant that God is offering and live life in covenant with him, our spiritual family, and our neighbors. But God isn't just asking for a momentary decision; he is asking for us to follow him as he has shown us—to literally give back all that he has offered in "life" and sacred living.

The gospel isn't a momentary decision of salvation, although salvation is a large part of it. It isn't simply forgiveness of sins, although repentance for abandoning what was given to us is part of it. It isn't the defeating of the fallen spiritual beings or the Satan figure, although them being bound is part of it. It isn't going to church, but the church is the bride of the Word. It isn't even just the great announcement of the forever King, although all these things would culminate and bring life through that King. It isn't merely allegiance, but this kind of sole allegiance is necessary, and without it, the gospel won't be found.

It comes down to the complete plan of the covenant—eternal life with God in his sacred kingdom. The story that starts with a sacred partnership in Eden has a plan to return to that way of walking in life with God almighty. A vocation of light, to be one with God Almighty and bear his very name and image.

The good news is rooted in our identity. We often say that we would like to see from the eyes of God. But have you ever considered what it means to be biblically seen?

Consider Genesis 16:13: "Then she called the name of the Lᴏʀᴅ who spoke to her, 'You are a God who sees'; for she said, 'Have I even remained alive here after seeing Him . . .'" (NASB).

Hagar lived a life of adversity. The Bible paints the picture as if she never had a glimmer of joy and came to the desert desperate. This passage is very interesting because it is one of the few places in the Bible where God seemingly comes into direct contact to a person. We get a relational feeling from the text that makes this revelation seem face-to-face. Traditionally we probably think that if you see the face of God then you'll die, but that's not necessarily always the case in the Bible (or at least it's complicated). Hagar here is seen by God and remains alive. The way that it's written in Hebrew seems to imply a two-way relational (face-to-face) encounter.

But what's interesting about the story is that she imagines that this is the end of her life (this is the implication that it is a face-to-face encounter), yet not only does she not die here, but quite the opposite; it is the renewal of her life.

Sometimes what you think is the biggest curse in your life can actually be transformed by God into the biggest blessing of your life. This is powerful transformational thinking rooted in the power of God. Usually when people hit an all-time low, they become open to plans of restoration. Brokenness can be the best agent to honesty.

In our American culture, we have likely become blinded to seeing things from God's perspective. Most of us admit that. But have you ever considered that in letting ourselves become blind to God that God in some ways may also become blind to us? God is always there to receive us with open arms, we know that; we never run out of chances to come back to him. But consider your relationship with God based on your relationship with an earthly best friend. What if you continually never called them back or made any effort to invest in their life? It would be a one-sided relationship. If you continued to treat them that way, at some point you would no longer be seen by them as a "best" friend. We are told that with God we are always invited to come to him or come back to him, but that doesn't mean there aren't consequences for our lack of relationship with him.

I always talk about patterns and consistency within the biblical text and that we should be alert to learn from them. Sometimes it is unfortunate how people view themselves: helpless, guilty, and inadequate; less than the people we could have been. This is likely how Hagar felt. Many have experienced the pain of Hagar.

People often try to paint a picture of who they want to be through social media. I always think it's interesting how people pretend to show a life that they might desire. In fact, they often spend more time trying to portray the life they want rather than on working toward the life they want. Don't fantasize about it, go live it.

Like Hagar, we often construct identities based on the expectations of others. Then there is another level of seeing. Just as Hagar discovered, we can be seen by God, and God sees who we can become.

Who are you? Do you know your identity is fully in God? He is asking you to pledge your complete life to this gospel. The calling is of his kingdom: all you have been given, and all that you are sacrificially giving back to him as it was freely given to you. He wants your complete heart, mind, and soul to follow him as a way of life; to fully honor and follow your King, Jesus, througout this earthly life and eventually

into the next. Too often we miss the mark and perhaps we even fall back into Old Testament-style defiance of God like Hagar did. My question is, where are you? Where is your spiritual family? Does your life resemble one who has become distanced from the Creator or one who is fully living the life and calling of the gospel?

*YouTube Expedition44 keyword search: Gospel*

CHAPTER 8

# A Covenant Mission

**Part 1: In the Beginning? | Read Genesis 3 and the book of Job**

> Seeing the Bible through the eyes of an ancient reader requires shedding the filters of our traditions and presumptions. They processed life in supernatural terms. Today's Christian processes it by a mixture of creedal statements and modern rationalism.
>
> Michael Heiser, *The Unseen Realm: Recovering the Supernatural Worldview of the Bible*

For the most part our culture has been trained to want everything in fast food, quick-and-simple style. I think I appreciate a straightforward, to the point, concise, description in some ways; but also, I occasionally appreciate slowing down and getting a more intimate or complete experience. That is essentially what this writing has been: in many ways it is just a simple summary that also provides ways to continue the journey for those who want to go deeper. This chapter is going to take a little bit more time. Most of us understand the stories of the Bible, especially the ones taught over and over since we were kids, but we often fail to make connections in order to understand how and why they are important together. This chapter is going to seek to summarize the biblical narrative. When we fail to see the big picture, we lose the intentional mission; we get caught up in majoring on the minors and lose the heart of the gospel from the beginning to the end. Perhaps we have known the basic Bible stories since we were kids but have never actually understood their role within the pages of Scripture.

The Bible starts by describing God's creation of the physical universe. Humankind on earth is the spotlighted creation. However, there is more to the story that we don't have the entire book or movie on. I like to say we don't have all the cards; we are missing some of the pieces. I remember when the first *Star Wars* movie came out when I was a kid. Everyone was a bit clueless because the first film started right in the middle of a galactic struggle that had been culminating for generations. But no one knew that until years later. Things that seemed like plot holes or weak problems in the storyline became apparent (or fixed) as the rest of the story was told over the course of many years. Part of the fun with the saga has been to speculate and figure out what we didn't know. The Bible may be read in a similar perspective. It might just represent the one movie that has been revealed to humanity. We have the story of our mission but we don't know a lot about the rest of the bigger picture that is likely connected to our story. There is a mystery.

There was spiritual life before the Bible, and likely a complete saga that we don't have access to. This is a huge part of our biblical story that most don't give merit to. Scripture gives us plenty of clues along the way. We have the divine council, the fall of nearly one-third of all the spiritual beings, a battle within a spiritual realm, and God's Son coming to earth in a cosmic act of grace that not only offers redemption to man, but in some way that we likely do not fully understand also binds the spiritual powers of evil in a war that ensues all around us—quite possibly a war over humanity itself, the treasure of the cosmos.

According to Scripture, we know that there were great multitudes created in a heavenly domain before our time. We often refer to them as angels or demons, but a better word according to the text is the "the holy ones," or those created directly by the hand of God. This mostly describes spiritual beings, but also encompasses the first acts of God's direct work of creation, namely humankind. Later in the story, others will be invited to also receive the title of a "holy one," but that will be a grafting into the community of holy ones, made possible through the cross by adoption based on obedient faith. Many of the holy ones will also leave or be cast down from this collective order.

This is worth stopping and thinking about. Unless you went to seminary and took a course called angelology, you probably haven't thought about this much, and what you have considered is likely based on fairy tales, not Scripture. We don't know how long these spiritual beings have been around, or what they did. We don't have that book. But we do know that part of their role, if not the majority of it, was linked to God's mission of the creation of those whom he would seek to have intimate relationship with. This human race would be created to, in its free will, choose to be part of his kingdom. In contrast, many of those spiritual beings, the holy ones of the heavenly dominion, would choose the opposite. Seemingly, also out of free will, they chose to rebel and fall or be cast down from the heavenly realm.

What's interesting is our biblical story doesn't start off by explaining any of this. What we know of it, we learn by picking up pieces here and there throughout "our story," putting together a few pieces of the puzzle at a time. In other words, it is not a main directive of the biblical narrative that was written for us to explain what took place before our story. We also know that there is more to come, and that God has some kind of vision for this that includes us and them grafted together. We only have our small story, with a very directed mission of covenant love. It is very much like watching the original *Star Wars* movie and then later finding out there are twenty other stories before and after it that are part of a bigger story. I hope someday we get to see, read, or perhaps even be figures in the rest of the saga. I feel like I am waiting for the next movie in the greatest trilogy of all of time.

When we read *our* story, the Bible, it is important to recognize the role that spiritual beings play. We often refer to the fall as the singular fall of humankind from the sacred garden temple called Eden. Few have made the connection that we are also likely reading the narrative of the beginning of the fall of the original spiritual beings as it is happening in Genesis 3. Have you ever considered that if the Satan figure had already fallen, he likely would not have been in the garden? There is so much we don't know here. But what we do know is that humanity fell, in part, because of the prodding of the serpent-spiritual being that had fallen (or was falling) as we read the narrative.

Have you ever stopped to ponder what exactly is going on here? Why the spiritual rebellion? Jealousy perhaps, due being replaced by man as the ones that would be intimate with God? And who is this falling figure in the form of the serpent? We often pin the classic "Satan" as a singular spiritual entity who can be traced from the fall all the way to the end of earthly days, but did you know that "Satan" actually isn't mentioned in the book of Genesis? Maybe we are giving too much credit to a singular being. The original term that we often use generically as "Satan" is a Hebrew noun that simply means an accuser, deceiver, or adversary. Sometimes in the Bible we see it used with a definite article (*ha-satan*), which seems to refer to a specific heavenly (spiritual being, perhaps even "holy one") accuser. The reason I refer often to this figure as "the Satan" is because that is how it is written in Hebrew (*ha* = the).

In the Old Testament we actually don't read much about a singular figure though. We get the idea of the accuser in a divine court primarily from the Book of Job, but that may or may not be the cosmic figure of evil that we always make him out to be. In fact, if I were reading the biblical narrative in its original Hebrew, fresh for the first time, I am not sure I would come to that conclusion at all. Is this a singular entity, or rather the combined power that represents the fallen spiritual world? This is going to challenge your traditional thinking. You're going to have a lot of questions. What about the temptation of Christ? What about the Beast? Personally, I believe that there is a fallen leader of the evil army, that the New Testament specifically refers to as "Satan." But in saying that, I believe we often read the pages of Scripture inaccurately, not recognizing the combined fallen spiritual beings as the complete entity of the evil adversary of God. These entities entice humankind and claim them for the world within a spiritual battle that persists. Their primary goal is to strip God's prized beings of their vocational calling to serve in his kingdom. If we miss this way of thinking, we miss a lot of "our" story. In the Old Testament we read of several fallen spiritual beings mucking up the world. Perhaps by the time the New Testament arrives, "Satan" has established himself as the clear leader of evil. Revelation would seem to imply that kind of thinking.

*YouTube Expedition44 keyword search: Deuteronomy 32, Job*

**Part 2: The Remnant | Read the Old Testament**

> God accomplished many things by having his Son become incarnate and die on Calvary. Through Christ God revealed the definitive truth about himself; reconciled all things, including humans, to himself, forgave us our sins; healed us from our sin-diseased nature; poured his Spirit upon us and empowered us to live in relation to himself; and gave us an example of what it looks like when we live in the kingdom. Yet, I believe all these facets of Christ's work can be understood as aspects of the most fundamental thing Christ came to accomplish: namely, to defeat the devil and his minions. He came to overcome evil with love.
> —Greg Boyd, *The Christus Victor View of Atonement*

Since the beginning of creation, God has offered covenant living to *everyone*—all who will believe and enter into faithful covenant relationship with him. This is true even during the time of Israel when God focuses his attention on his chosen people. That's why we have stories of those outside of Israel coming to faith and even finding themselves in the bloodline of the Messiah. The big question we like to ask is who will be saved? Churchianity has become fixated on the concept of salvation, but the truth of the matter is only God knows the answer to this question. The biblical narrative wasn't written for those wanting a get out of jail free card, it was written to the those willing to commit their entire lives to faithful living. This is and has always been the central theme of the story. Throughout this account, we find that in the end this will not be many. The road is narrow. This is the remnant, and this relationship is holy, set apart, remnant living.

But even within remnant thinking we find ourselves continuing to look at salvation as a prize. What if it isn't? What if salvation is part of the promise but it's simply just one of the elements. Maybe the call of set-apart living is a bigger picture. The Bible often talks about jewels, crowns, jobs, and roles of ruling in a recreated heaven. Maybe in our salvific thinking we are missing the big picture. Regardless, the remnant is a major part of the plan.

God created man and he was good, along with the rest of creation. But this creation was not perfect. Man would be in partnership to serve and walk with God to organize and complete the creation. Man was incomplete and thus was completed by the creation of woman to live with him in a joint partnership with man and God. Together they would have a divine relationship with the rest of what God had created. The covenant was simple: "Don't eat of this tree." Whether you completely pin this on humankind or give more merit to the fallen spiritual being(s), humankind would break this covenant and be cast from the garden.

From this point on we see the beginning of a downward fallen spiral, a mucked-up earth. It's also what appears to be the beginning of the cosmic spiritual battle that would be fought over humankind. Within a few pages of our story, evil has nearly taken over all the earth—and not just once, but over and over again. God first sends judgment by flood and destroys all that is evil. Many grapple with this, and some have even left the faith over it. How could a good God destroy many that "must" have been innocent? As the story continues, we will continue to ask the same question as God sends his people to go to war, killing hordes of those around them to gain the "promised land." How can we be in a story of God's divine desire to have a love relationship with all the world yet seemingly be so quick to destroy much of it?

The story when viewed as a whole will answer this great question, but let me just briefly touch on this so you can be thinking this way from the beginning. Consider this, perhaps new, way of thinking of the Old Testament story. God's plan is for anyone that chooses him. Period.

This is shrouded in a cosmic grace that we can't fully understand. We are asked to simply believe in the person and character of God and his plan for all humankind. We don't understand the vision, the timing, or the structure; and it has not been given to us to understand. That is the paramount of what it means to simply walk in faithful obedience to the God of the ages. But let me just give you a clue. What if the plan for humanity is bigger than what our human minds can fathom? What if the victory is far greater than what we ever considered? Is that kind of thinking too big for God? What if the spiritual life of one person who was given physically to the flood could, through some great powers, actually have been won? What if our conception is actually backwards or upside-down; what if, rather than being destroyed as we think in our human minds, they are even given eternal salvation through this work and the work of the hand of God to come? We don't understand this kind of backward thinking. It is not human or within the worldly wheelhouse of comprehension; it is spiritual thinking. For now, I just want you to simply consider this. We will return to this question later in the book. For many this will raise an eyebrow of concern, but please bear with me. (Trust me here that I am not referring to any hint of pluralism or of all roads leading to God.)

From the flood we have a covenant with Noah not to destroy the earth in this way again. In the same way the story began in Eden, Noah is told to repopulate the earth. I think God hopes for a rebirth of free will decisions to fully follow him in covenant living. Humanity grows and we are given a table of nations. Don't you find this interesting? Maybe you have never considered it. Why does the Bible stop the story to give a genealogy? The answer is in the next chapter, at the Tower of Babel. The Bible uses the word *nations* to describe humankind. The story of Babel is often misunderstood. This is where I have to stop and introduce an idea that I refer to as Deuteronomy 32 thinking. You may need to watch one of my videos on this or possibly read the book that I quote from at the beginning of this sub-chapter. After the flood, the fallen spiritual beings are still at work with humankind. And again, we don't have this story. It is part of our story but not written in full in the book that we have been given. But we do have enough to reckon what is happening. It seems that the nations are allotted to some of the heavenly beings to help God rule over them. Many think that this was supposed to have been the royal, priestly role of humankind in the garden, but that plan crumbled. When you read the story of Genesis 11, we find the people creating a ziggurat-like tower so that they can make a name for themselves and not be scattered. Essentially, they want to be equal to God. Nimrod is hunting God.

In the Old Testament we see God speaking to others in the heavenly realms regularly. In this case we read, "Come, let *us* go down." (NASB) There are several places in the Old Testament where we also read this: Genesis 1:26, Genesis 3:22, Genesis 11:7, Deuteronomy 6, and Isaiah 6:8 to name a few. When God says these things, he is likely speaking to the spiritual beings. There is reasoning for the Trinity here as well, but it seems the better hermeneutic is to simply give merit to spiritual beings working with God. It is likely a dual Hebraic idea. In its original context the audience would have understood the text to be referencing what they knew—the divine council—but it is also possibly a reference intended for later, to show where the Trinity could be found in the Old Testament. This way of thinking doesn't by any means discredit the Trinity; each situation should be dealt with hermeneutically on its own basis.

In terms of the tower and the table of nations, it seems that at this point in the story God chooses to let spiritual beings manage some of the nations. As this happens, the people, in likely every case, begin to worship the spiritual power over them, not Yahweh. We don't have the timing, but it seems that these spiritual beings fall or are cast down as God chooses to focus on one nation that will be his portion: the nation of Israel. Eventually the spiritual beings are worshipped as gods and challenge Yahweh. All of them seem to fall.

Am I saying that every other nation fell? It seems that way, but I take this back to the divine plan, so, bear with me a moment through the rest of the story. Immediately after Babel, we read that God calls Abraham and makes a covenant with him to the nations called the covenant of circumcision. I believe that Abraham kept this covenant, but his offspring broke the covenant. This is a non-conditional covenant though, meaning God said without any qualifications that this would happen. Even though humankind would go on to break the covenant, God did not.

We are introduced to a number of archetypes within the biblical narrative. Although this can be controversial or argued, an archetype is a symbol or example that represents something, often something to follow. Adam is an archetype of man, Abraham is the archetype for the human with the most faith, and Sodom and Gomorrah are archetypes or pictures of extreme evil.

As many know, reproduction links the blood structure of humanity. The Bible doesn't explain the science of this, but God designed life this way. Life is in the blood and carried on through reproduction. The covenant is for generations and the life is given in the blood, the spiritual cutting of the blood covenant between man and God made in the physical form of circumcision in the Old Testament and would similarly be signified for the new covenant by baptism into the Spirit. This is spiritual, communal living in both the Old Testament and the New Testament. We aren't just asked to consider our own personal relationship with God, but also our spiritual family.

It is apparent that during the story of Abraham, evil is rampant on the earth. This doesn't seem to ever go away. Sodom and Gomorrah are destroyed but within a short time, that kind of evil is again rampant, in nearly the same form and even in the same place. This is a reoccurring theme throughout the Bible. We read the story of Joseph and get the idea that few were following Yahweh. Throughout the story of a rampantly fallen world, we read that God remained faithful to a remnant—those who chose to follow him.

And then, generations later, God chose to focus on one nation for himself. The nation of Israel would be Yahweh's chosen portion. He makes a new covenant with Moses for the nation of Israel specifically. This covenant was conditional based on the people following the law he gave them. He wasn't abandoning the nations; he still had a plan for them. As we continue to read how these nations were conquered and fell to the sword, I encourage you to consider that they may not have been completely lost but actually given redemption—as backwards as it may seem. God would use his nation to eventually offer salvation to the world, to give redemption to those who would choose him throughout all time and all nations. This happened in a way that we didn't and still don't expect or see. This kind of backward thinking is a central theme of the entire biblical narrative. To many reading the story, it seems like God only wants one group of people, but behind this plan is the bigger picture of redemption to redeem all nations.

God led his people out of Egypt in a miraculous way, but immediately we see that Israel wasn't faithful to Yahweh. This is the heart of the narrative of the Old Testament, and it continues even after God focuses his plan on a small group or singular nation to be set apart as the nation of the priesthood. They continue, in their free will, to choose to follow the world or even the evil spiritual powers that have fallen and are being worshipped as gods, rather than the one true God. God's amazing love and grace to them does not change despite their unfaithfulness. This is his non-conditional covenant to the nations for the redemption of humankind shining through the broken conditional covenant of Moses.

If you're really thinking through the story with me, you have to ask at this point in the story if this was what God wanted or had planned. We seem to think of God's power as controlling everything. Some theologies would tell us that all things have been set since the beginning of time and executed as God's perfect plan for humanity. I can't help but think that God's plan for Israel was meant to come to fruition and regain the nations by a faithful covenant with him. Yet that never happens; the covenant is broken over and over again and eventually God gives them over to judgment and exile. Does this make God less omnipotent? By all means no! It continues to show that what God desires more than anything is for intimacy in a relationship that is chosen out of free will. It is dynamic love. Perhaps God's omnipotence and destiny are a bit more dynamic than you have ever considered.

Many get the law wrong. It wasn't merely six hundred-plus laws to follow completely if you want to be holy. It was a course of action, a plan for generations greatly influenced by a fallen world to stay on track toward an intimate relationship with God. Many see it as a stopgap until the Messiah would come and give life through the blood that had been lost. Even though Israel would be lost and scattered (the Diaspora), a small remnant would remain, the faithful who continued to live a life set apart, wholly devoted to covenant living and intimacy with God. Through this remnant would come the Messiah, who would give life to not only those to come, but those who had come before. The cross runs both ways, giving life to those that were lost.

Can we fully comprehend what the cross accomplishes? I don't think so. We get clues that the thief would be in "paradise," which is an Old Testament term usually associated with a holding place similar to hades. We don't read that people are going directly to heaven or hell in the Old Testament. This should tip us off. If Christ sees the thief on the cross immediately after death, it means that Christ is going to see those in paradise. Many evangelicals cringe at the idea that Christ also may have visited hades while in the grave. The Apostles' Creed has many times been written off by those struggling with that line. Does Jesus visit both paradise and hades to possibly preach and give a second chance of salvation to all that have previously fallen short? Could the power of the cross be so great that it gives an incomprehensible salvation? This would seem quite backward to our concept of justice, yet would fit a love so great. Am I saying that all will be saved? To be clear, I would love to see universal salvation for everyone upon this second chance preaching (in the Old Testament and possibly within the New), but I am also not going to put God in that box; in him all things are possible. I have to admit, there are some struggles within that theological framework that would be hard to reconcile within the complete lens of Scripture. We will get to this, but the concept that many may find salvation is better supported in Scripture than many think. However, we don't have these cards; we simply are told to live completely for him in obedient faith. But isn't that also one of the goals of the Bible? That all might know? Could and would God find a way to make this happen? It's hopeful thinking.

When the thief on the cross is told he will be in paradise, the end of the Old Testament covenant is being fulfilled. From this point on, it seems these places of paradise and hades are no more. Heaven becomes the intermediate place for those who believe until the Messiah returns and establishes his eternal kingdom, a recreated heaven on earth. What about those who don't live in obedient faith? In the New Testament we are introduced to the concept of hell. Some will say that we also read of it in the Old Testament, and that may be true in a far-reaching sense. But in the New Testament we get a feeling of finality of judgment that encompasses this word. It is a different sense from that presented with Sheol or hades in the Old Testament. In the same way, we are introduced to this intermediate state of heaven in place of paradise or Abraham's Bosom. At the cross, the game seems to have slightly changed.

I have found that God's nature doesn't change from one testament to the other. What was true in the Old is true in the New. The Old often works in the same way as the New, and oftentimes foreshadows it. Our human minds can't see the big picture though; that hasn't been given to us . . . yet. I have stopped trying to figure out salvation. It could be given to only the few, the remnant; it could be given to many more than we thought possible. But the narrative we are given doesn't encourage a belief in momentary salvation that culminates in a pie in the sky type of reward. The narrative describes a completely set apart way of life, fully and wholly devoted. A line of royal priesthood, walking with God into the eternal kingdom. That is the calling of the remnant.

*YouTube Expedition44 keyword search: Circumcision, remnant*

## Part 3: The Scapegoat and the Power of the Blood | Leviticus 16, John 19

> At the end of the day, these rituals were aimed
> at healing the fractured relationship between God

and his people, so they could become the kinds of humans he made them to be. In the same manner, Jesus' death provided a permanent way for people to be reconnected to the presence of the living God despite their failures.
—Tim Mackie, *The Bible Project: Old Rituals and New Realities*

In our culture one of the hardest things for a person to understand about the faith journey is the connection to blood. I have to admit, in most cases when you tell the story of a God that desires blood, it sounds very much like a vampire story or ancient ritualistic cult. Why is the God of the greatest love story of all time seemingly infatuated with blood? If God is the author of the story and is all powerful, he could have based what he wants of humankind on anything; why blood? These are the sermons we aren't hearing on Sunday mornings in seeker-sensitive churches (or likely any mainstream service), and it is unfortunate. This is a huge part of the story.

As you can imagine, the understanding of blood in Scripture is paramount to our ability to know what God asks of our sacrificial lives. If our lives exist to enter intimate relationship with God, and what he wants is linked to blood, shouldn't we seek to understand this heavenly desire? Yet, it seems a little strange to us in our modern world. However, in the culture it was written in, it likely would have not been perceived as strange in any way. Blood was a regular part of ancient culture; we see it in nearly every dimension of ancient life. Let us also not forget that this is not our home, and that our spiritual understanding should be of a different dominion. To fully answer this question, we have to tell the story of the old covenants before we can understand the new covenant that was given just for us.

When God makes a covenant with Abraham, it is based on circumcision and is a foreshadow of a covenant to come. We still use the phrase today that we are going to "cut a deal" with someone. This is language found in the Bible and refers to the metaphorical "cutting" of a covenant. Whether it is circumcision or the ancient tradition of blood exchanged in a handshake, there is something in the blood. Why?

In both the Old and New Testament, we have a central theme that our faith encompasses more than just you and me. In the Old Testament we understand this to be a responsibility for all of our brothers in a sense of communal obligation. This message is grafted into the narrative early on in stories like Joseph's. It becomes a central theme written into the law, as well as in relational story upon story throughout the pages of the text. In the New Testament, Jesus teaches the same principle (to love your neighbor) as paramount. As we live this way with those around us, eventually it will permeate the nations; this is the great missional calling of discipleship. The covenant with Abraham is far-reaching. It begins this love covenant that will know no boundary. It is foundational to the life that God desires of us.

When we hear a sermon on the sacrifice of Abraham it usually leaves us questioning God's motives, and some perhaps even walking away from the faith altogether. Its sounds so crazy. God is going to ask Abraham to sacrifice his own son to him? What kind of God would do that? What kind of father would even consider this? This sounds like a monstrous, bloodthirsty god. It sounds so messed up according to our modern conception of human love. So backward. I have four boys, and in my rational, human mind, I would never, ever offer up one of my boys in a cult-like sacrifice to some god. Right? That's the way we think.

So, let's figure this out. Abraham is the archetype of complete faith in the biblical narrative. In other words, there is none greater. If there were a man of greater faith then we would have that story, but we don't; Abraham was that person. But still, we continue to think, "What kind of God would ask, or even consider, a father to give up his greatest love?" The basis of such a notion is incomprehensible to most, to the point that, according to our finite minds, it sounds like the opposite of love—it sounds crazy. But when we read this story as the "archetype" of a man with the greatest faith of all time, it makes a little more sense. Could the man with the greatest faith of all time trust God that much?

The reader should be thinking this way! In our culture we are afraid to go here! What if a father could give up something he loved so much; what does that look like? How can a love that strong exist? Our minds are uneasy. This is how the covenant story to redeem all nations began. This is also how it was won—by the blood of the cross—and it will culminate, beyond our understanding, in the coming of the Messiah. The sacrifice of such great life is in the blood. This is truly beyond our human reason or understanding, yet God's grace gives spiritual peace. Abraham would have made the sacrifice, but God doesn't ask him to; he is simply setting the table to foreshadow the future sacrifice that would be the redemption for all mankind.

The Abrahamic covenant message is very similar to the covenant relationship God would offer to Israel. When God chose his portion (the people of Israel), his expectations were based on the law that he gave. The law was a picture of the love that would be given for them and the life that is in the blood. Those coming out of Egypt were serving many gods. They needed a law to help them understand how the one true God would be different from the other gods they had previously served and given life and allegiance to. They were used to gods that they served for a purpose: if the gods were honored by them, then the people were blessed by fertility, long life, or good weather for farming. If the gods were not appeased, the people would suffer through pestilence or even plague. Yahweh was different. He wanted a relationship with his people. He wanted to tabernacle with them in life. This is essentially what it meant to walk with God; but it was foreign to their thinking. It seemed backwards to them.

Leviticus 16 explains the Day of Atonement. This is a phrase that goes back to the saving of the people in Egypt, the story of the blood on the doorposts. Notice from the beginning that God asks for blood to be spread over the entrance to each home that will be claimed in his name. Even before the people understood what they were claiming, the blood had the power of redemption. Have you ever considered this? How might this impact your theology and in what context does it agree with the rest of Scripture? These are the kind of questions we need to read Scripture with.

God asked them to remember that they were covered and set apart with sacrificial blood. Each year from that point on, they would give the best portion of their time, treasure, and talent to honor and remember what was done for them. (There were three feasts when the Hebrews were to gather together according to Exodus 34:23, when the high priest would intercede communally on behalf of all the people. These feasts were based on upright living in the eyes of God and they took precedent over everything else in life. They were celebrations in the name of godly living.)

The feast began with the high priest going through a series of ritual cleansings. This was a picture of the holiness that God desired in order to walk with them, together in their presence. There is so much to this; there is significance in nearly every part of the law and how it relates to honoring the Most High God. Unfortunately, this book will not describe everything, and I encourage you to dive deeper. This is a rich continued picture of sacrifice.

A blood sacrifice is used to atone and/or cover. It costs something; it has great worth. To those in Israel, the best of what was available and offered or given to them by Yahweh were the animals. The animals were not only a sign of life, but they also provided for the basic needs of the people (food, work, transportation, etc.) and were a sign of provision and wealth. There was a feeling that if you honored God (or even gods) in your life you might be rewarded. This is called the retribution principle, and as we learn in the book of Job, isn't necessarily the way God works, but there may have been some adherence to it in and through the eyes of God. Culturally within Israel, many understood it to be this way. God asks for what means the most to people to be given back to him. It is a continuous cycle of grace that keeps on giving. God desired that man would freely offer the treasure of his heart back to the glory of God. Blood represents the giving of complete life. But there is more to this idea; there is a sacrifice and there is an offering for atonement. Leviticus 16:7–10 says:

> Then he is to take the two goats and present them before the LORD at the entrance to the Tent of Meeting. He is to cast lots for the two goats—one lot for the LORD and the other for the scapegoat. Aaron shall bring the goat whose lot falls to the LORD and sacrifice it for a sin offering. But the goat chosen by lot as the scapegoat shall be presented alive before the LORD to be used for making atonement by sending it into the desert as a scapegoat.

Aaron would bring forth a second goat and lay his hands on this goat while confessing the rebellion of the Israelites. Then the goat was sent off into the wilderness. We often dwell on the forgiveness of sins with God. In fact, everyone reading this book has at some point in their life considered the forgiveness of their sin against God as a step to accepting the free gift of salvation. This way of thinking may be more of a construct of man than of God. God doesn't dwell on the sins of our past, present, or future. He never has, and we are told in covenant that he never will. He desires that we honor him, and that means to live a righteous life. But when we read passages of forgiveness, such as this one, they are nearly always describing sins against God. Our primary directive from the beginning of Scripture to the end is to love God with all we have been given, putting nothing before him. Forgiveness is important in a pursuit of holiness, but it isn't the only ingredient.

In the Old Testament, the explicit commandment was to have "no other gods before me." We always like to reword this in our new covenant thinking or somehow discredit the Ten Commandments. We make this out to be "gods" of work, or TV, or something worldly. While I can understand how these things can separate us from completely living for God, that's not really what the first commandment or idols meant in the culture in which this was written. God from the beginning to end wants to be the lord of our lives. There were and are other spiritual beings vying for our allegiance and lives, and God commands to have nothing to do with them. This is the main directive.

It isn't some fairy-tale idea of confessing every time we sin so that we may gain salvation. The mission is unwavering allegiance to God. Forgiveness is part of that right relationship with God, but likely in a different way than you might have it framed. When Aaron sent the goat into the wilderness, it wasn't to cover the swear word someone from the community said in malice when they stubbed their toe (although it likely took on that power as well); it was far greater-thinking. It was a covering of grace for them when they were disobedient to the vocation that God had created for them to be fully invested in. Without this vocation to walk obediently with God, they were missing the point of creation itself. This is big-picture thinking: living for the blood of the Lamb.

You might have heard this part before. It has been mentioned in the Mishna that during this service the Hebrews would take a cord that had been stained red by the blood sacrifice, symbolic of their disobedience to their life calling, and place it on the head of the scapegoat. The cord would be briefly placed on the goat but then would be removed and used to tie the veil of the holy of holies. This would be symbolic of their sin of disobedience that had continually separated them from life with God. It was said that throughout the year this cord would turn from blood red to white; that God would look past their sins and, in his grace, see the purity and intention of a faithful heart (mind and soul). But tradition would tell you that year after year, as the heart of Israel wandered, the cord often didn't turn to white. Eventually the temple was destroyed, but later other temples were built, and the sacrifices were reinitiated. The story of the cord isn't recorded in Scripture; you must dig deep into ancient writings to find it. But like many extrabiblical sources, this one gives us hints to better understand the story that God has given us about how forgiveness is linked to blood.

(To be clear, the Bible is complete. We need nothing more than Scripture to have eternal, intimate life in Christ. But I have read many books—some written hundreds of years ago and some written just a few months before I read them—that have helped me understand Scripture and my calling.)

According to Leviticus and oral tradition, there was a man appointed to lead the goat into the wilderness. The word in Hebrew for the scapegoat is *ahzahzel,* which carries with it the idea of "taking away." As you can imagine, no Hebrew would ever accept the responsibility of leading the communal sin against God into the wilderness. A gentile would be hired for this job.

I imagine the process became quite cumbersome year after year, and eventually God's chosen people completely lost the traditional ritual of holy cleansing in addition to what was being asked of them by God. The one thing God asked for first and foremost was obedient, faithful, allegiance to him, and the Israelites failed. Time after time they continued to worship other gods. Eventually God gave them up into judgment by captivity. The temple was destroyed and God's people were enslaved and scattered. Eventually some, the few, the remnant, returned to ask, once again, for faithful covenant living with God. They asked that they might be delivered from their lives of bondage and return to freely living completely for God as their king. They longed for the days of being completely allegiant to God in the theocracy he had originally given his people. This remnant returned to faithful devotion once again, asking God to be the giver of life.

God continued his faithfulness to give the remnant something. The prophets began to share the voice of God: that redemption was coming, that there was hope of a Savior. I am sure what they desired was earthly. They wanted a spiritual force to fall on their captor, and for the Lord to deliver in battle, just as he had led them many times before in the stories of old. But what they got seemed backward to many.

Remember the story of Daniel? He was a remnant. He oversaw all the wise men from the East; they would have been looking for a sign of deliverance and of a king. One day the star appeared. Many of the writings of Daniel foretold this, nearly to the day. God had given the remnant something to place their hope in, something that would once and for all cover the sin and disobedience of the people who were intended to be set apart for something sacred. Somehow, outside of all our human understanding of justice and grace, the God of Abraham would once again offer a new covenant.

Fast forward to John 19. We pick up in a story of the Messiah, the Christ, the Lord of all who comes to give life within a kingdom. Yet none of this looks familiar. How can this be the Savior? It seems so backward. Jesus's own people gather before Pilate to say he is guilty. They cry out, "Take him away," and the Roman gentiles lead him to the cross. Do these words sound familiar? What about the crown of thorns around his head resulting in what looks like a scarlet ribbon over him, as the people were likely chanting the same words from hundreds of years before: "*Ahzahzel, ahzahzel, ahzahzel.*" Hebrews 10:11–14 says,

> Day after day every priest stands and performs his religious duties; again, and again he offers the same sacrifices, which can never take away sins. But when this Priest had offered for all time one sacrifice for sins, he sat down at the right hand of God. Since that time, he waits for his enemies to be made his footstool, because by one sacrifice he has made perfect forever those who are being made holy. (NASB)

Before Christ passed, he shared with the remnant, his faithful disciples, that he wanted them to continue this oath of allegiance to a coming kingdom and that he would rule as the Lord of all, regathering the nations to himself. And when he died, no one could understand what had happened. We still struggle with this today. We don't know the full work of the cross; we don't need to. We know that it was the power to save. The veil separating humankind from God was torn and the cord fell once and for all. The blood of the cross would run both ways. The plan to enter into a holy covenant with God would be not only restored but made perfect. The new covenant was cut; the plan of redemption for all humankind was fulfilled. Nothing more than obedient faith to walk with God would be asked for. This commitment would encompass all of life, the heart, the mind, and the soul.

Why blood? To humanity, life is in the blood. It is a symbol of what we hold most dear. Jesus was both the sacrificial lamb and the scapegoat. He is everything we need for life. In this new covenant we are given the choice out of our free will to vow our lives in faithful obedience and become "sons of God." Do you remember that term? That is what the Old Testament uses for those created directly by the hand of God. You see, we are adopted into the kingdom family as faithful heirs. In Rome adoption was held higher than natural birth. If you naturally birthed a child, they could be disowned at birth, but once you adopted them, legally they were completely within your family. When we confess and give our hearts to Jesus as the Lord of our lives, we are given the blood of the Lamb that signifies life at its fullest. We are remade, born from above, into the light-bearing, vocational person that God originally created us to be. To walk with him and partner with him in this lifelong calling into the eternal kingdom. In the same way he sacrificially gave his blood that we may have life, we can now sacrificially return this gift of grace in the form of life. Not only are we new creations but the blood of the Lamb is in us. Our bodies are the temple of the Holy Spirit, set apart to live to our fullest potential for the kingdom. The reciprocal dance of grace.

But what of the gods of the Old Testament? We are told that they were bound at the cross, but we don't have a full understanding of what that means. That may be in the story of another domain. What I do know is that the evil of the Old Testament is still vying for the lives of all; that the battle still wages.

As we look at the way the Old Testament foreshadows the New Testament, we might also pick up something about the second coming of the Messiah. The Bible tells us that no one knows the time or the place. This in and of itself should probably dispel any notions of trying to guess how the Messiah's second coming may happen. What we do know is that we are simply called to live for the kingdom today and that we do not need to worry about tomorrow—as we cast our cares on him, the author and perfector of life to its fullest.

*YouTube Expedition44 keyword search: Leviticus 16, scapegoat*

---

# CHAPTER 9

# Heaven on Earth | Read Revelation 21 and 2 Peter 3

The idea of "heaven" as the eternal hope of the righteous has no structural place in the story [of the Bible]. It is simply irrelevant and extraneous to the plot. Heaven was never part of God's purposes for humanity in the beginning of the story and has no intrinsic role as the final destiny of human salvation."

—J. Richard Middleton, *A New heaven and a New Earth: Reclaiming biblical Eschatology*

Our culture is so fixated on dying and going to heaven when the whole Scripture is about heaven coming to earth."
—N. T. Wright, Surprised by Hope

I have found that many people's view of heaven is a bit scripturally off. I have alluded to this already. Most largely have a Platonist view of the soul leaving the body and going to the pearly gates and streets of gold, where we grow wings and sing forever.

The biblical authors thought of heaven and earth more in terms dual dominions of God's creation, but not the only dominions of his creation. Consider spheres that occasionally overlap. For instance, you might have a heavenly domain and an earthly domain. Eden likely is a great example of these domains overlapping. The material met the spiritual. Most people think in terms of God delivering people from earth into the heavens upon the death of a life well lived, but this notion is actually pretty hard to find in Scripture.

In the Old Testament, God's people were asked to walk by faith in Yahweh. Those that did seemed to go to paradise, or "Abraham's bosom." Jesus was the bridge from the old covenants to the new; when he died on the cross, he told the thief that today he would see him in paradise. This has confused many. Was this heaven? Scripture doesn't give us all the answers. The best we can do is make an educated guess according to the rest of Scripture. Perhaps the faithful were held in paradise because there was not an adequate sacrifice to fully cover them until the work on the cross, specifically the resurrection. At the cross those in the faithful holding place may finally have been delivered to heaven. That is what it seems to suggest. But this heaven isn't described as the final destination, but rather an intermediate resting place similar to that of paradise in the Old Testament. This idea seems very clear when Jesus tells us that in his Father's house are "waiting" rooms.

The final state is when God brings heaven and earth together in a great act of re-creation. This is the completion of our biblical narrative in the book of Revelation. What starts as walking with God in Eden will end with a similar picture of God restoring us to be royal priests in a sacred place involved in his sacred work. The complete cosmos will be joined.

When we discuss spiritual domain, we need to keep in mind that in some ways this is incomprehensible to the human mind. We want to touch and feel everything. Heaven does not have literal geography; it is immeasurable. We can't even fully describe it because our language is of humanity, which doesn't have the words to express the heavenly dominion. How can we even start to have a conversation about something that we simply don't have the words to express?

Over and over, we have attempted to put God in a box, but God is not spatial. The Word became flesh "and dwelt in our midst." This is a reference to God dwelling with the first Israelites. The word for "dwelt" is best translated as "tabernacled." God is omnipresent but often chooses to appear in a specific place or to a specific person or peoples. In the Old Testament this was often in the form of a cloud, but also in other ways (such as a burning bush). This is often described in Scripture as God "revealing" himself. In Revelation we see a picture of the final state, where a New Jerusalem comes down to earth and God will inhabit all.

In our culture it feels like few really know God or what his plan is or how his character is truly revealed. Let me introduce you. God's name is Yahweh. The tetragrammaton is the four-letter Hebrew word יהוה (transliterated as YHWH). All the books of the Old Testament (except Esther, Ecclesiastes, and the Song of Songs) refer to God in this specific way. It is sad to me that we have lost this sense in the English translations.

Traditional observant Jews would not pronounce the name of God or read it out loud. They would replace it with other names or forms of the name for God, such as Yehovah (Jehovah), Adonai, or Elohim (although this one makes me cringe as it is literally simply "gods") to name a few. I prefer the Most High.

The name of God is given to us in Exodus 3:1, where Moses asks God what he should be called. God's reply takes some working through for most people in modern Western culture. In Hebrew it is *Ehyeh asher ehyeh* or, translated, "I am that I am" or "I will be what I will be." This is based on the simple letters YHWH which originally (like all letters in the Hebrew script) indicated consonants. (Vowels are seldom written in unpointed biblical Hebrew; the marks were added by the Masoretes several centuries later to assist reading.)

Then to make it even more complicated, in Hebrew we have several situations where it seems God is personally revealing himself yet using different names, such as the term *malakh YHWH*, which occurs sixty-five times in the text of the Hebrew Bible, and can be translated either as "the angel of the Lord" or "an angel of the Lord." This is a fascinating study.

You might also be familiar with the usage of *Abba* (Hebrew word *'ab*). As Scripture unfolds from the Old to the New Testament, this becomes more frequently used as the opposite to the term "the Satan." In the same way, we most often we see the definite article *ha'ab* ("the Father").

Yahweh God created everything; he alone is sovereign; there are no other gods; he has no rivals (even though, as I have explained, there were other spiritual beings that were being worshipped as gods). Thus "Father" in Hebrew signifies the most high. To call God "Father" is to use covenant language depicting the Father of all the originally created "sons of God" and those recreated as sons and daughters by their adoption into the covenant.

Once you recognize this more personal covenant language throughout Scripture, you can't stop seeing it. Remember the story of the Exodus? Playing on the word *son*, God told Pharaoh through Moses to let his son (Israel) go, or he would kill Pharaoh's son. Another example is in 2 Samuel 7:13–14, when *son* is used for the kings of Israel. This is the beginning of the Davidic covenant, which would bring the seed of the Messiah, offering all to enter into the kingdom. "The Lord said to me, 'You are my son, today I have begotten you'" (Psalm 2:7). Every anointed son of David could claim the title of "God's son."

So now that we understand the role of the King and that we are the kingdom, we need to understand the place and the position of the kingdom dwelling.

Some believe that the Bible implies levels of heaven. Some have said three, others seven. There isn't a lot of framework for this in Scripture; it's mostly dreamed up as a construct of man. The closest thing we have is possibly the Old Testament tabernacle as a foreshadowing or picture of heaven. Nearly everything in the tabernacle represents something within the later biblical picture. The mosaic is seen as a gradation of holiness within the temple (i.e., the outer court, the holy place, and the holy of holies). Perhaps similarly, 2 Corinthians 12:2 may describe three levels of heaven. But even within this thinking we need to consider that God may simply be the domain of pure holiness himself and that the other "levels" might be layers that are simply closer to his revealing presence. The entire biblical narrative is essentially a story of God's love to bring humanity back to walking with him in the fullness of his sacred space. This way of thinking is a central theme in most orthodox Christian beliefs.

In the end, the ultimate hope in Jesus Christ is completed in God's new heaven and new earth, which are often underemphasized or not known at all by Christians. Many want to see heaven as a prize of salvation, but that kind of thinking is hard to find in the text. The joy we experience through life in Christ on this earth seems to foreshadow our joy made complete by walking in the holiness of God's perpetual sacred domain. Perhaps on this earth we get glimpses of heaven. We know very little about heaven or the recreated final state of heaven. Some have considered the intermediate state as more of a joyous sleep or hibernation but again, these are thin interpretations with very little scriptural bearing. We simply don't know exactly what the grand plan is.

Heaven-on-earth thinking is not only about the final state of living with Christ, but also enthralls our current life, over which he reigns from the heavenly throne. Live for the kingdom today. Everything is connected. We don't know a lot about heaven, but I am pretty sure we won't grow wings and sing hymns forever and ever . . . I think it is going to look a little bit more like what we know of Eden, and I hope we have pets!

---

Consider your heritage. The God Most High desires for you to be his family. Live for the kingdom here and now in the position that God has given you and with the gifts he has enabled you to continue giving back to his kingdom, that all of who you are may represent the sacred name of YHWH.

*YouTube Expedition44 keyword search: Heaven*

CHAPTER 10

# Hell

God is not wrath. Though we may rightly understand and describe the consequences of divine consent to our own self-destructive will as the wrath of God, the truth remains that God is not wrath; God is love. God is not a bloodthirsty deity requiring ritual killing. Though this may have been the only way we could understand God four millennia ago on the lower flanks of the holy mountain, the truth remains that God is not bloodthirsty; God is love. God is not violence. Despite the fact that religion has a long history of sacralizing violence by projecting it on God, the truth remains that God is love. God does not operate an eternal torture chamber. However we understand the state of a postmortem soul incapable of love, the truth remains that God is not a sadistic torturer inflicting eternal pain; God is love. God is not a killer. Though many have misread the book of Revelation to such an extent that they think God's final solution for sin is the "Final Solution," the truth remains that God is not a genocidal killer; God is love.

—Brian Zahnd, *Sinners in the Hands of a Loving God*

My memories of growing up in a mainstream, rather large, evangelical church often evoke the idea of endless altar calls "scaring the hell" out of people to try to get them to make a momentary decision of supposed salvation. Go through the four or five easy steps and pray the prayer and you will be saved from everlasting burning in hell, then put a rose on the piano to commemorate the decision. I imagine many have had similar experiences. I find stories like these of American church culture to be problematic within the lens of Scripture.

God is love and offers a covenant to intimately walk with those who enter into a decision to sacrificially live for him in faithful obedience to their humble kingdom calling. This is the primary directive found over and over through the pages of the Bible; any message or ideological thinking contrary to this missional calling is not biblical. There are many "Christian" doctrines that are founded on cobbling together bits and pieces of the text that do not fit with the major theme of the Word. If your theological framework involves focusing on a singled-out verse (often taken out of context), or even worse, is based on non-scriptural tradition, you might want to identify these issues and rethink them. This kind of theology, or lack of it, is rampant in our church culture, and unfortunately routinely preached from pulpits across the country.

Let's set the table by discussing some questions that often arise relating to our view of hell. What kind of a God, who deeply loves those whom he created, would ever will them to be burned alive forever and ever? Is this a God of extreme love who desires all to find life, peace, and truth in an intimate relationship with him, or does it describe a fictitious version of a monster God who will inflict unending torture on all those who don't choose to enter relationship with him? Understandably, God is God and can do whatever he wills; but what has he promised us in his Scripture? In order to understand the concept that is presented as hell in God's Word, we first need to come to a realization of who God is and what he is offering to us. God's character and the concept of hell, theologically, will agree since they are both part of the kingdom framework and design that God has given us. Is your understanding of the character of God within the pages of Scripture filled with grace, love, and mercy, or is it a picture of a monster God who in the end desires to forever torture the masses of humanity whom he has claimed to love?

It may seem strange that I am phrasing what seems to be a very simple question this way, but it can actually be quite complex. In the Bible we have a few different terms that are associated with hell: Sheol, hades, gehenna, Tartarus, and the lake of fire. Each have a different meaning and context, yet in our modern church culture we usually lump them into one place or idea.

Hell is the generic word we typically use to describe where people whose names are not written in the Book of Life will be cast after judgment. Sheol is an Old Testament reference to a dark underworld place. Hades is the New Testament reference to Sheol, or possibly to a place very similar. Gehenna is an earthly place that seems to take on figurative references to hell during the time period surrounding the life of Christ. Tartarus is mostly referenced as the lake of fire in extrabiblical Second Temple-period literature. And the lake of fire is where evil will be cast when the Messiah returns and claims victory.

Our understanding of Sheol is complicated. Some verses in the Old Testament seem to describe it as a place where all the dead will go as a holding place, while others, especially reflected in later literature, considered it to be the home of the wicked dead. In a similar view, paradise is the home of the righteous dead until judgment (e.g., 1 Enoch 22; Luke 16:19–31). To make things more confusing, the Talmud associates Sheol with gehenna. When the Hebrew scriptures were translated into Greek around 200 BC, the word *Hades* was substituted for Sheol, and seemed to give continued precedence for this usage. There is good evidence that they are the same thing. Some have argued that in the Old Testament the holding places were needed so that after the cross Jesus could come back to minister to them before they met their final destiny. This argument suggests that we don't know if this same picture fits what happens after the cross. Since believers seem to go to heaven immediately, even before judgment, what happens to those that are not clearly with God? Do they go into a sleep state or a Sheol-like holding place as we read in the Old Testament? Scripture gives hints to these questions but doesn't seem to clearly give us the answer.

The term Tartarus is the most interesting as it technically does not exist in Scripture, but we seem to gather a great deal of our mainstream view of biblical hell from this word. The word does exist many places outside Scripture within the corresponding culture that the New Testament was written in. In the New Testament, the noun *Tartarus* does not occur but *tartaroō* (ταρταρόω, "throw to Tartarus"), a linguistically rather strange, shortened form of the classical Greek verb, appears in 2 Peter 2:4; but this is also arguable. There are 686 hapax legomena (a word or phrase of which only one instance of use is recorded) in the New Testament, 54 of which are found in 2 Peter. That is a lot for such a small book, and scholars are mixed on how to handle much of 2 Peter (and Jude for that matter). Because of this singular reference, some scholars distinguish Tartarus as a place for wicked angels on the basis of this verse, which leaves us to question if it is simply another word for the lake of fire (which I will get to, and which has a more clear understanding within Scripture.) Tartarus occurs in the Septuagint translation of Job into Koine Greek and in Hellenistic Jewish literature from the Greek text of 1 Enoch, dated to 400–200 BC. This states that God placed the archangel Uriel "in charge of the world and of Tartarus." Tartarus is generally understood to be the place where two hundred fallen Watchers (angels) are imprisoned. (Watch the "Deuteronomy 32" Expedition 44 video for a better understanding of this.) Tartarus is also mentioned in Plato's Gorgias (c. 400 BC), as a place where souls are judged after death and where the wicked receive divine punishment. Many of our thoughts on hell are more closely tied to this kind of Greek mythology than they are to what the Bible actually says. This is a problem. What does the Bible actually teach on hell, and is it different than what Greek mythology has conveyed to us? As a side note,

I would agree that the New Testament writers were very familiar with, and often even quote, non-canonical uninspired works that influenced their thought.

The English word hell comes from Norse pagan mythology in the form of Hele, who was the god of the underworld. In the early 1600s, King James Version (KJV) translators applied this word to all four or five of these related words in that translation. Sometimes in the KJV the word is used to denote a physical place on earth. This is the framework for gehenna in the Sermon on the Mount. Gehenna was a valley outside of Jerusalem, better described as the Valley of Ben Hinnom (or the Valley of the Sons of Hinnom; see 2 Chronicles 28:3; Jeremiah 19:2–9; Jeremiah 32:34–36). We regularly do this sort of thing linguistically in English when describing or alluding to figurative living situations. In the New Testament Judaic mindset, the term *gehenna* also carried a context of the underworld, or someplace where good people would never want to find themselves (in the English language and American culture we might say, "The other side of the tracks"). It is also worth noting that the pre-gospel context of gehenna is not necessarily presented as an afterlife idea but the idea of being overcome by one's enemies in life. We see God allowing this as a form of judgment—for instance, the Israelite exile, captivity, and Diaspora. In the Old Testament and culturally throughout Second Temple context, gehenna had no connections to afterlife thinking. This picture of gehenna is of an earthly judgment or figurative language of the worst circumstances on earth. Wrong or right, we have associated eternal hell with gehenna because of our judgment thinking and the way we frame our understanding of situations that may foreshadow the eternal concept of hell on the physical earth. In a similar fashion, C. S. Lewis framed shadows of joy on earth as pictures of eternal heaven.

The last phrase we have for hell, the lake of fire, is likely the best one of the five from which to gather a scriptural understanding of eschatological thinking. When we consider the more westernized concept of hell that most people have today, it is perhaps based on platonic understanding (described previously) that has been applied to Revelation

20:10, 14, which mention the lake of fire as the place into which the devil and other cosmic evil entities will be cast. We find out a little bit more in Matthew 25:41, where we read that the eternal fire is specifically prepared for the devil and his angels. As we go back to Revelation 20, we continue reading that death and hades will be thrown into this lake, thus denoting that they are separate dominions from the lake of fire itself. Revelation goes on to say that those whose names are not written in the Book of Life will also be thrown into the fire.

The Old Testament doesn't provide this full picture. As I have said many times before, the Old Testament contains the story while the New Testament gives clarity to the things mentioned in the Old. The authors didn't have the whole concept or understanding, and God's story is focused on its overarching mission of redemption—not on explaining every detail. He meets people where they are and uses them within the kingdom regardless of their knowledge base. Sometimes this has included divine revelation of spiritual things, but often it doesn't. The writings (original manuscripts, which we admittingly do not possess today) were simply inspired (which you might find means something different than you always thought it to mean). As we read of prophetic foreshadowing in the Old Testament, we go to the New Testament to find the completion of the story. Then, beautifully, the New Testament goes full circle and also sheds further light on the original Old Testament concept. In this way, the New Testament functions as a commentary on the unseen revelations of the old covenant. In terms of understanding, it often feels as if the Old Testament is a cup only half-filled with water. The New Testament is the cup filled.

Ancient covenant keepers studied Torah, which led to reverence, and reverence led to faithful allegiance, which developed a relationship of holiness with God. In the same way, the Old Testament is connected to the New Testament, and we are given a similar mosaic to the connection of study leading to intimacy with God as a circular relationship of holiness. The way the Old and New Testaments connect circularly is, in essence, a direct reflection of our relationship with God.

As we approach these texts on hell from this platform of under-standing, we read that the lake of fire was created as a place for evil, fallen spiritual beings. Following this thinking, Revelation 20:14 seems to allude to the idea that the original plan for humankind walking with God got mucked up, and now some of these people who won't be in the Book of Life are also going to be cast into the lake of fire with the fallen spiritual beings, those original created sons of God that have fallen or been cast down. It is almost as if this book began at the fall to keep track of coming judgment. We continue to read about the eternality of life with God in the future recreated heavens and earth; traditionally, we have then applied the same kind of eternality to this lake of fire. This implication is found less in Scripture than people think when they re-ally dive in.

Who is Satan? I think Christians often give the devil too much cred-it. We have made this entity out to be the singular cosmic bad guy that is almost equal in power to God. If you started in the Old Testament and read through the pages of the Bible in one sitting, you probably wouldn't frame the picture that way. Our traditional teachings of hell (and fictional books and movies) have influenced us toward this con-clusion. Better scriptural thinking is it to consider the Satan figure of the Bible as one of the fallen spiritual beings, who likely (from the nar-rative of the Old Testament to the New) rose to lead those fallen beings in practices contrary to things of God. Revelation 12 connects several of the common terms such as we find in Genesis 3 and Isaiah 14. This brings clarity to some of the other Old Testament terms like the di-vine rebel, serpent, and possibly the accuser of Job. Going back to the concepts of hades or the underworld of the Old Testament, we don't necessarily get the idea of fire when we read about them. What we do read is that this underworld is where the disembodied spiritual beings (including those described as Anakim & Rephaim) are given domain. There isn't even a hint of some that are righteous having a hope of being "saved" from this place.

Whatever your framework or understanding of hell is, Scripture does make it clear that a person who has never had an allegiant relationship with God (resulting in a journey of action defined by faithful obedience) is essentially separated from God and will experience a place referred to as hell in some capacity (although some may even challenge this, such as within an Orthodox view of hell, which I will get to). On this earth they are separated, and as a result (unless there is divine interaction in the afterlife), after judgment, they will also be separated from God in the coming spiritual domain. The great majority of Christians can all agree with these statements regardless of one's view.

There are three (and arguably four) basic views on hell that are compatible with evangelical Christianity. Surprisingly, when you get past the surface, they are all similar and affirm the fundamentals of Scripture. All of them find a common thread and agree that unity with Christ in eternity can only be attained through obedient life in Christ based on Jesus's sacrificial atonement on the cross. All the views also affirm that there will be judgment of life lived while here on earth.

I want to emphasize that when we are having a conversation about finality, it is important to remember that we as humans are not to judge. This is reserved for God himself. You may notice that when I talk about what the Scriptures say is necessary for eternal life, I speak carefully. There is no checklist, steps, coupons, or warranties for sale in the pages of Scripture that will guaranty your everlasting life. As funny as this sounds, many constructs of man have attempted to build the concept of salvation into something that is either not present at all in Scripture or that would require some pretty far-fetched imagination.

As I have suggested earlier, God by his very nature defines justice. Man wants to shape what justice should look like by our earthly standards and courtroom culture, but according to God, that is backwards thinking. God is the definition of justice. There are views of hell that have been framed with this kind earthly thinking that disagree with the Bible. For instance, the Bible is clear that hell exists. To arrive at some kind of thinking that there is no hell doesn't fit within the framework of Scripture.

What is the final state of separation from God for those who have not walked faithfully with him and have not been judged faithful to rule with God into eternity? There are many different names for these different understandings and interpretations of hell, and several subtle differences that I have found debatable. The three main views of hell are eternal conscious torment (referred to as ECT), annihilation (also referred to as conditionalism or conditional immortality), and universal reconciliation. There is a fourth view called the Orthodox view of hell that I will also briefly expound on. I have listed these beginning with what is traditionally taught and accepted in mainstream Christianity, then leading to the lesser-held views.

There are several passages that describe consuming fire, others that describe utter destruction; some use the word *perish*, and others simply use *death* to describe an eschatological end or some other figurative language that seems to point to an end. You will see these words in these passages, which are often used to support various views on hell:

- Psalm 1:4–6; 37:20, 34, 38
- Matthew 3:12; 7:13, 19; 13:40
- John 15:6; 3:15–16
- 1 Corinthians 3:17; 15:22
- 2 Corinthians 2:15–16; 5:22
- Hebrews 6:8
- James 1:15; 4:12; 5:19
- 1 Thessalonians 5:3
- 1 Tim 1:10

## Part 1: Eternal Conscious Torment (Traditionalism)

The traditional and most common view of hell, particularly in America, is eternal conscious torment (ECT). In fact, if you have ever heard a theological teaching on hell, it is likely that it was within an ECT framework. The average churchgoer simply assumes that this is the only scriptural perspective of hell. Ironically, I would also argue that this view is actually the most difficult to frame within Scripture itself, from the perspective of the totality of Scripture and the narrative love story of God for his creation. ECT is based on seven verses in the New Testament (John 3:36; John 5:28–29; Matthew 13:40–50; Matthew 25:41, 46; Mark 9:43–48; 2 Timothy 2:15; Revelation 14:9–11).

ECT has been the predominant view since the Reformation. Augustine, Thomas Aquinas, and John Calvin are usually associated with this view. This view holds that all humankind are immortal beings. After the final judgment, the souls of the damned will be cast into the lake of fire. Therefore, everyone will live forever in a conscience eternal state, either with God or separated from him in the lake of fire. Those cast into the lake of fire will be in a state of anguish or torment that will never end. Essentially, God's wrath and justice need to be satisfied by punishment; since God is eternal, then the punishment is also eternal. Believers will be in a state of forever bliss and, therefore, it is usually considered within this doctrine that God will, in his omnipotence, wipe away every tear. This carries the connotation of possibly erasing memories of loved ones cast to hell—that the heart of the believer would be reconciled to a sense of justice for those in forever anguish when seen from God's point of view after judgment.

The main scriptural proponents of this view are Matthew 25:46, where we read, "And these will go into everlasting punishment," and Revelation 14:11, which has similar language. Most are surprised to find out that the main tenets of this concept as previously illustrated come more from Greek mythology then they do from Scripture, but admittedly you *can* frame it this way, and many have. Unfortunately, this view is likely one of the main reasons that people have walked away from the Christian faith: they can't reconcile this doctrine of wrath with a God of love, and thus have completely dispelled evangelical Christianity.

ECT is usually presented as God (from a sense of justice) teaching people a lesson by holding them in never-ending anguish to get even with them for not choosing him. Often within Calvinist (Reformed) theology, unconditional election is considered to be one aspect of predestination in which God chooses certain individuals to be saved. As if this description of God doesn't sound bad enough, this doctrine, when added to Calvinistic thinking, maintains that man didn't choose God, but instead God chose who would go to heaven and who would be destined to hell. It becomes a lottery: who will be tortured by God and who will win the golden ticket?

Eternal conscious torment is described as the ongoing, painful wrath of God coming to fruition upon those who have been judged and found "guilty" (as this is usually framed in a courtroom type of scene) during their physical lives. These beings will be kept "conscious" or "alive" and tortured in the lake of fire, with no end. Essentially their judgment is final, with no longer any chance of restorative grace and/or end (annihilation) of their anguish. This is understood as a permanent state of forever torment. On taking this view, you need to come to the realization that when Scripture uses the terms *dead* and *death*, it does not mean (ironically) the traditional definition of "ceasing to exist." In other words, all are immortal beings.

This understanding of hell seems sadistic. If this were true about the character of God—that he is going to simply torture people forever and ever for the sake of getting even—then by our typical understanding (both within a spiritual and a carnal worldview) he would be seen as the greatest monster ever. We often frame Hitler as the worst person to ever exist for killing millions in the gas chamber. But when you put God in these shoes, choosing to send the majority of those he has created into excruciating torture forever and ever, that makes Hitler seem pretty mild. Hitler's extermination of a few million Jews happened pretty quick in a gas chamber, it happened relatively quickly. In this way of thinking, Hitler annihilated millions and God would send perhaps billions to hell. Hitler would use a gas chamber bringing death rather quickly compared to God who, in this view, would torture people forever. This kind of torment thinking doesn't seem to line up with the Bible's general message of God's loving character.

The most difficult issue with this view is that Peter, John, James, and Paul all describe divine judgment, but not a divine causation of *eternally lasting torment*. It also seems to take the most "massaging" or "theological gymnastics" to make work. Typically, this doctrine or view aligns with systematic theology and not biblical theology. Biblical theology is focused on studying a portion of the Bible and taking into account its relation to the rest of scripture. For instance, if you are studying the building of the temple in Nehemiah your going to want to see what led up to the event and then see the connections and lessons affirmed in the rest of the Bible and the New Testament as they reference the re-building of the Temple.

Systematic theology is focused on many portions of the Bible that seem to discuss the same topic or subject matter. For instance, it could be a study on the character of God or references to a cloud.

These methods of theological study can be complementary, but are often viewed as different categories within scholarly interpretation.

It is more of a construct of man than it is a construct of biblical thinking.

When we approach Revelation 20 and read that the fallen spiritual beings will be tormented "forever," the text goes on to say that others will be thrown into this fire; however, it leaves out the "forever" part when mentioning the others who are thrown in. Jude 7 speaks similarly of everlasting fire (everlasting is a better translation than eternal; only God is truly eternal). However, when we study this passage, we find that it says Sodom and Gomorrah were served a punishment of everlasting fire. It uses the same words as Revelation 20. Yet we clearly understand that Sodom and Gomorrah are not still on fire. It is clear that this is figurative language, and if we interpret it that way here according to what we do plainly understand, it makes sense to translate Revelation (which is more ambiguous) in the same way. Throughout our American culture there is a feeling that hell is a state of finality, but when you really start working through each passage you probably won't arrive at a clear thinking of "forever burning" without a little help from Greek mythology. I must pause here and say that this premise seems to be based on the world's thinking and likely not the intention of Scripture or godly thinking. That said, it has been accepted as the predominant view in evangelical Christianity.

A lot of the popular phrases that you've always heard associated with hell such as "weeping and gnashing of teeth" are used within the constructs of ECT. I have found that most (if not all) of them are biblically presented as figurative language. As I have mentioned before this is core to a Hebraic way of thinking.

The last consideration is to simply work through the logic of the text and doctrine. We simply don't think about the Bible enough. Are people saved or lost by chance, as Reformed doctrine would say? What about those that are unborn, or those that have not come to the age of reason? What about those that have not been given the same chances to consider the gospel as often or to the quality that others have? Do they go straight to hell, as church tradition and most of ECT has taught?

What about the urgency to receive the call to walk with God *now*? The Bible regularly emphasizes an urgency that seems to imply that those that come to God now will gain something. Is it simply salvation, as the ECT camp suggests, or the construct of jewels in your crown and/or a closer proximity to God within a ruling state of heaven? We don't have the clear answer to this in Scripture, but it obviously shapes people's doctrine regarding the final state of existence.

What we do know, despite our personal views, is that God is constantly at work to reverse the effects of the fall and walk with us once again in a completed and renewed kingdom. We know that God is light and that there are echoes of light everywhere revealed in natural creation within our earth that lead to a true understanding of Jesus.

## Part 2: The Problem of Evil, and God within the Context of Hell and Eternity

I find it fitting after a section on the problems within the view of eternal conscious torment to also take a moment and speak to one of the other huge questions of faith within Christianity. As I mentioned, many walk away from God entirely because they can't reconcile ECT, thinking it is the only view of hell within biblical Christianity. The other main reason people walk away from God is their inability to come to terms with God in the context of the pervasive evil within our world. They are two very similar subjects.

Often when we get to an area within the Bible that is hard to make sense of or where the answers don't seem apparent, I have found that the best way to reconcile our understanding is to see what the rest of the Bible might say. Sometimes this takes a bit of research and digging. I am going to give you an example of this type of exegesis, both as an example of hermeneutical study and also to help answer this question.

To help us understand a future that is not clearly revealed, it may help us to understand the past, which *is* clearly revealed. Typically, what is true of God in the past will also carry over to the future. We don't know why God allows all the evil that exists in the world. We know that it is contrary to his very being and we know that he is omnipotent and therefore could stop it. So why doesn't he? Throughout the Bible we see evil that God allows, and occasionally evil that God decides to end. We don't know why God sometimes allows evil to continue and sometimes chooses to put a stop to it.

With this question comes another that is very similar: why does God seemingly allow, and perhaps even cause, violence in the world? We read stories of God killing thousands in battle—mass genocide. How can a good God of love and mercy be so violent? I think in answering one of these questions we will find the answers to all of them. The great majority of the passages people struggle with are those concerning the Israelites and their slaughtering of the surrounding nations, namely the genocide directed at the Canaanites.

Let's take a closer look at the story. God promised Abraham the land many generations before Israel was created. God's covenant to Abraham still exists while God chooses his portion Israel to regain the nations. God's adapted plan for Israel still involved the same land, which would eventually, by grand design, claim back the whole earth (Psalm 24:1; 1 Corinthians 10:26). Yet for over four hundred years, the land had been inhabited with people that were emphatically evil and anti-Yahweh.

Many people, when talking about the problem of evil, ask, "Why does God allow all this evil to happen in the world?" and, "Why does he not put a stop to it?" I hear people asking that question all the time—as if they think that they are somehow qualified to question the morality and doings of God. But what is interesting about the story of Israel and the Canaanites is that we see a situation where God was patient for four hundred years and *then* decided it was judgment day. It is one of the times in history when God actually chose to *not* allow the evil that pervades the world, and instead utterly decimates it.

The Canaanites were particularly evil. Sometimes we get stories in the Bible of extreme cases. Abraham, as we have mentioned, is our example of extreme faith; the most faithful archetype of all humanity. In the same way, the Canaanites are our archetype of the most extreme evil. Just to give you an example, one of the things the Canaanites would regularly do was offer their babies as sacrifices to Molech. It is unclear whether Molech was actually the name of the god or the description of the style of sacrificing babies to any foreign god; either way, we see it as the extreme archetype of evil.

It has been recorded by the Greek writer Plutarch that when they offered the babies as living sacrifices to be burned to death, the drummers would have to pound their drums so loud that you couldn't hear the babies screaming. The statues resembled an incinerator with arms outstretched; the babies would be placed on the arms to suffer a slow, horrendous death. What I want you to note is that God obviously had a major problem with this. It is presented as the archetype of *extreme evil* within the entire context of the Bible.

Why would God allow such evil? Well, in this case he didn't. He said it needed to be completely annihilated. As you can see, there is a conundrum. Many ask, "Why does God allow such evil atrocities to continue on earth?" But then, if God destroys such evil, as he did in the case of Sodom and Gomorrah and Canaan, people say, "Why is God so violent?"

Let me urge you to step away from the narrative and just think about our discussion of hell as framed within ECT. If God shows torturing defenseless humanity as a picture of the most extreme evil humanity has ever encountered, do you really think he would choose to do the same to those who didn't choose him? If the Bible says that this torturing and killing of babies is the archetype of evil that God utterly condemns, how could he turn around and then do the same to those that don't accept him? Isn't that a huge contradiction of character?

Some look at the Molech sacrifices and think that God will judge those people in the same way that they judged their own babies. In our culture we often call this "an eye for an eye" thinking, but that kind of framework is largely out of context in the Bible. The biblical perspective seems quite the opposite when representing the character of God and the upside-down kingdom that Jesus was framing when he taught the Sermon on the Mount. I personally can't equate the character of a loving, merciful God to sending the unborn to hell.

And what about our own nation? Are we a godly nation? In many of the same ways, we continue to offer infant sacrifices. Is this a picture of a godly nation or a picture of a nation that God abhors for this kind of evil? The mosaic of evil was shown to us in the Old Testament and our nation may not be far from it, or quite possibly, may have already surpassed it. We are probably killing more babies than the Canaanites did. I sure don't want to be around when our nation hits the four-hundred-year mark based on this. Or maybe I should better say, I want to make sure my allegiance is on the right side when that day comes. How long will God tolerate such killing?

So, when people ask, "Why doesn't God stop extreme evil when it happens," my answer is usually that their view of God won't change whether he does or doesn't. We have to come to ultimate acceptance that God is just in his judgment and Jesus is the definition of love and that together they are the same person.

Before I move on, going back to the views of hell; I need to bring closure to this idea of the problem of evil. As this book has shown over and over, Hebrew writing is very much figurative and needs to be understood that way within the Hebrew cultural dynamic. We look at the bloodshed of the Old Testament and say things like how barbaric it was, but is it really much worse than what mankind created at the beaches of Normandy? Yet much of the world is very much okay with that story, reckoning it to the name of freedom and justice (and maybe we should be).

When the Old Testament speaks of annihilation situations, it is often with figurative language. Ancient Near Eastern culture often uses hyperbolic language; for instance, in Deuteronomy 7 we read that God says to wipe everybody out. But then right after that it says don't intermarry with them. How can you intermarry with them if they're going to be completely wiped out? In the case of the Amalekites, the Bible states many times that they were "wiped out or annihilated" but then we read of them again and again. In 1 Samuel 15 Saul kills all of them. But then later, in 1 Samuel 27, it says David kills all of them. How would David kill them all if Saul already did? Then to top it off, guess who kills Saul? An Amalekite! They obviously weren't all dead. This language was hyperbolic. I would venture to say that when we read of the killing of "men, women, and children" that it is a similar situation, and could even be a Hebrew idiom as it is a rhythmic phrase in Hebrew resembling a pun. I think it is better understood as simply a picture of definitively winning the battle.

We see this a lot today in our English language and culture and we're fine with that contextual understanding, but then for some reason we have a problem when the Bible does the same thing. For instance, in sports today I might say my ten-year-old son's soccer team totally annihilated the other team. Did they "totally annihilate" them? Did my ten-year-old take out a sword and cut all the heads off the rival team and stand at the center of the field with a bloody head in one hand and a sword in the other exclaiming, "I am Reid the mighty warrior!" at the top of his lungs? No! That would sound insanely barbaric of my ten-year-old. Well, in the same way, the Bible uses the cultural language of the time. Now, some have a hard time with this because they don't want to discredit a biblical story. If we start admitting that figurative language exists, where do we draw that line? I think when the Bible describes the exact details, it likely happened. There very well may still be situations of graphic bloodshed that took place in the name of God. Did God tell Israel to act as they did or did the people act on their own? The

Bible is filled with stories of godly people, such as the disciples, who walked with Jesus but often still didn't understand what he was really desiring of them. We see this even more prevalently with the Israelites in the Old Testament. Many, both in Scripture and today, claim to be acting in God's name but have actually been and continue to act in a way that is far from the heart of God. Instead of representing the image of God, they represent God in vain.

In every situation we need to hermeneutically explore the text and apply the best exegesis based on what we have. Sometimes we get illustrations of annihilation where it wasn't literally complete annihilation; other times we get stories like the flood where people were so evil that God literally said we need a total reboot and that if we don't, this evil is going to continue to pervade the world (at least if you adhere to a global flood and not a local one.)

There's one last consideration here, especially since this discussion falls within the chapter on hell. There is a feeling within the text that sometimes (particularly when read in Hebrew within that cultural context) when God annihilates people in the Old Testament, he may essentially be exhibiting sacrificial grace. I have danced around teasing you with this notion a couple of times early in the book.

This is a bit of a foreign idea to us since we don't recognize or fully understand the cultural dynamic. In the Bible, the primary Hebrew term for sacrifice is *qorbān* (something brought forward, an offering). We often miss the connection that at the end of every battle this sacrifice was made to God. The sacrifice was given for all that had fallen. Essentially, everyone who had been ushered into the next life, enemy or not, was offered to the Lord. We know that they went to a holding place such as hades or Abraham's bosom; and in this sense, we have the understanding that they might still have been given another chance to place their faithful obedience to the Lord. This comes back to the idea of Jesus returning to preach to them during the three days following his death.

These *qorbān* sacrifices are the foreshadowing of living sacrifice. We often say that in his justice, God gives life and takes away life. One of the reasons why we seem to be okay with that is because there's more to life than just the physical life; there is the spiritual and what some people refer to as the afterlife.

The way God annihilates people in the first death as a measure of grace, giving them a second chance to come to him (at least in the Old Testament), may foreshadow the way the second death offers a similar gift of grace and mercy eschatologically. What seems to us to be an act of utter bloodshed from man's modern view of an ancient culture may, in God's eyes, be an act of his complete loving grace. Throughout the Bible narrative, we see times where the course of events is not Gods ideal way, but he meets people and cultures where they are and still offers gifts of unending mercy. Perhaps with some of these violent passages in the Bible, we may not see God smiling, but we still see him adapting. We get this sense when God initially establishes his rule in the theocracy of Israel but then grants them a king to make them like other nations, seemingly knowing that it would be the beginning of their demise.

In some ways we can recognize that God is the supreme entity of justice and judgment, but he is culminated in the ideal picture of love, grace, and peace—in Jesus. In the Old Testament, the world's way was to be met by bloodshed, violence, and war. In the new covenant, God seems to adapt to this kind of thinking and sends Jesus as the ideal measure. Even in Revelation, when we're hoping that Jesus completely annihilates the evil people of the world, we see the sword coming out of his mouth—which means it's probably not going to happen the way we think it's going to happen. It continues to be upside-down kingdom thinking.

In the end, God's nature must be reconciled together: both the violence of the Old Testament and the culmination of Jesus. As I stated at the beginning of this section on hell, our view of hell (or of godly violence) must be rooted in our view of God's character. God is intelligent and purposeful and has an intricate plan and design. We need to inquire as to what specific purpose God had in creating hell or in reconciling the violence of the world. His character is revealed in all of his acts. Thus, we learn about God through what he has made and what he does.

## Part 3: Annihilation / Conditional Immortality

The next view on hell is annihilationism, which is also called conditional immortality or simply conditionalism. There is an argument that at some point these terms represented slightly different views, but currently within theology it seems as if everyone is happy to accept these labels being used interchangeably as the same thing.

Those that take this view are going to interpret words like *perish* in John 3:16 to actually mean a state of finality. *Death* essentially means utter death in texts like Romans 6:23. You also get a sense that terms such as *destruction* have a finality to them. 1 Thessalonians 1:9, 1 John 5:11–12, 2 Peter 2:6–7, Philippians 3:18–19, and Hebrews 10:39 and much of Psalms would be interpreted as destruction, framed as an end of life both in a physical sense but often spiritually as well. Many of the notable early church fathers held to this view, including Irenaeus, Ignatius, Athanasius, and Arnobius.

There are a few basic tenets that this view holds. Only God is immortal by nature (1 Timothy 6:16.) God grants life eternal on the condition of faith in and through him (John 3:16, 10:28; 1 John 5:11–12). They would also claim that throughout Scripture, those separated from God after judgment are never declared to be immortal. The terms *destroy*, *consume*, *perish*, and *death* all carry a sense of finality. Another aspect that is worth considering within this view is that suffering is not eternal (Matthew 11:22–24). The punishment may be eternal or irrevocable but not the suffering itself, as described in texts like Matthew 25:46. This view also seeks to better address the problem of sin in the universe that the traditional view of hell doesn't seem to reconcile very well. Within annihilationism, the lost will be resurrected for final judgment and upon their condemnation will be thrown into the lake of fire (literal or figurative) and cease to exist, perhaps following the appropriate amount of punishment. This view also possibly handles the Scriptures about the forfeiture of eternal life by those who rebel against God the best. Many modern scholars such as Edward Fudge, F. F. Bruce, Ben Witherington, Greg Boyd, and Chris Date have concluded that, with an unbiased pursuit of hermeneutics, this seems to be the most reconcilable view of Scripture.

So, let's discuss some of the thoughts shaping this view. Scripture speaks of finality, and it means something by it. Those within ETC would say that if you do not accept the free gift of salvation, you will be cast into eternal conscious torment in the lake of fire. Many Scriptures seem to indicate that at some point God is going to have had enough; either a person (or people) turn to him or they don't. In the Old Testament when God had had enough, we see the word *wrath*. This simply means that God gave the people over to something. His hand of providence was removed.

The basic understanding of annihilationism is that after judgment, if your name is not found in the Book of Life, you will be cast down to hell, resulting in the final destruction of your being. This makes sense from our human perspective of physical life and might work the same way within spiritual life. Most who hold this view see it as a literal lake of fire where death comes quickly (and you might even say mercifully), and those earthly beings cast down are annihilated. This is usually understood to mean completely dead immediately, but some frame it in terms of appropriately timed judgment within a state of anguish.

If God has created hell to be the place to end spiritual life, the earthly parallel makes sense as the second death in scriptures such as Revelation 2:11, 20:6, 20:14, and 21:8. Within this view hell is essentially a temporary state, but carries the idea of ultimate finality, or permanent non-existence.

Despite the ability to understand and accept this view of hell, some struggle with the idea that everyone who goes to hell receives the same final annihilation. That may not seem fair. As I have implied, there are several different variations within conditionalism to account for this. Occasionally some conditionalists might argue that after judgment some may experience hell longer than others, but then are simply annihilated. Revelation seems to imply that the fallen spiritual beings may be tormented longer than the earthly beings that have turned from God. Others may simply say that God's judgment can't be reconciled in human conditional thinking; that God can and will exercise both grace and judgment in a sense of rapid finality of final death. That if a "soul" is cast into a lake of fire, all of it will be quickly consumed. This fits very well with many Scriptures that also identify God's nature as a consuming fire.

If we go back to Genesis 2, to the story of Adam and Eve, we get the picture that as long as they continue to eat from the Tree of Life they will have everlasting life, but when they fail to eat from that tree and are cast out from the garden, they become mortal. They will no longer have the gift of life. God's gift of eternal life was removed by his own hand. In the case of expulsion from the garden physical life is the result; following life on earth, the result would be a finality resulting in eschatological spiritual death. When a spiritual being is with God, they are given everlasting life, but when they are separated from God, death is the result. To frame it differently we are not intrinsically immortal; living forever is conditional upon belief in Jesus Christ. Physical death foreshadows spiritual death.

As a side note to this thinking, some have questioned that if the garden was supposed to have been an eternal state and this gift of immortality could be taken away could that foreshadow the sense of eternality also given in heaven? Most assume that heaven will last forever. There becomes a question of eternality, or whether "eternal" in fact means forever. As I mentioned earlier, many will argue that only God is truly eternal.

Within Scripture, the overwhelming majority of texts regarding judgment speak in words of finality, such as ceasing to exist. Annihilation thinking seems to best fit these passages.

One of the other main reasons to consider annihilation is where Scripture mentions "death of death" in 1 Corinthians 15:50–58, Isaiah 25:8, and Revelation 21:4. If death is truly destroyed then it's hard to understand any kind of unending conscious torment. In the view of annihilationism, the separation from God is permanent. But, in terms of reconciling the major message of the Bible with the love and grace that God continually offers, the idea of a "just" but complete ending of life in annihilation may actually exhibit a good deal of grace.

Another minor variation of conditionalism is that some may experience hell in a similar way (whether by literal flames or, more likely, as a figurative description) but will be given another chance to receive Jesus. Some will choose to and some will not, and those who do not are simply annihilated. If you fall within this minor view of conditionalism and understand the passages that imply a continued opportunity (or unending) grace to be reconciled with God, you arrive at the question, "Is God's grace ever used up?" According to most within the annihilationist view, eternal punishment would simply be death, leading many to wonder if this is creating an injustice. That no matter what sin you have committed on earth or how bad you were, everybody simply receives the same end. Thus, some are coming to believe that there may be another chance for reconciliation with God in a sense of refining fire. In this view such a person may experience a taste of hell, but if they place their faith in Jesus, they are accepted and given an opportunity to live spiritually. Since in the new heaven and new earth we get the idea that some of those who originally placed their faith in Jesus may rule over the angels, it could mean that they also rule over those who ultimately decide to place their faith in Jesus after judgment and an experience in hell. Much of this is just a construct of man's thinking, as we simply don't have clear answers within Scripture. Within this view, God's grace concerning decisions to follow him does not cease after judgment. We see God in his mercy continue to offer restoration. This variation continues to line up with similar thoughts of layers or levels of heaven; perhaps those that are granted heaven within this condition may only be in the outer realms of heaven. Some will go be reconciled back to God and sent into the heavenly realm and those that do not will simply and finally be annihilated.

Thus comes an idea that some may experience hell and still come into the kingdom after placing their newfound faith in Jesus. This idea gets very close to the third view (and some would argue that it actually is a subgroup of the third view) which is universal reconciliation. If you start to think this way, it might lead you to wonder why, if some may be reconciled after judgment through a merciful yet omnipotent God, can't everyone be reconciled? Is your God that big? Could the pages of Scripture regarding judgment work within this understanding?

## Part 4: Universal Reconciliation

Ultimate or universal reconciliation (or restoration) is the theological view that all people (and possibly fallen spiritual beings) after "death" will eventually be reconciled to eternity within the presence of God. Many will experience hell (and again this may be literal fire or could be figurative) after judgment, but all will eventually be saved. Given enough time, possibly burning, and having met Jesus in judgment, what person wouldn't come to this place? It is also interesting that Isaiah 45 and countless other passages state that every knee shall bow, and every tongue shall swear allegiance. I bet this phrase practically jumps off the page to you by the end of this book as seemingly stating what is required for eternal life in Jesus, which is obedient, allegiant faith.

Many of the early church fathers would have held this understanding, including Clement of Alexandria, Origen, Gregory of Nyssa, and Gregory of Nazianzus.

I feel the need to pause and preface the understanding of universal restoration or reconciliation. This theology is not to be confused with universalism in the context of all gods leading to the same road. That framework is better described as pluralism, but some will argue that universal reconciliation may open the doors to that kind of thinking. In our Western minds we have often aligned the two, but they are different in that the universal view of hell is still framed around the belief of the one true God, Yahweh as described in Scripture. The other universalist belief of pluralism, which people are more familiar with, is a complete contradiction of Scripture. You can't claim that Jesus is the Messiah and the sole giver of life and also accept the teachings of other earthly "gods." This was the predominant message of the law—that we should have no other gods before him.

Essentially, universal reconciliation holds that God desires all to be saved. That is pretty hard to argue from texts such as Ezekiel 18:23, John 3:16, 1 Timothy 2:4, and 2 Peter 3:9. Scripture also seems to at least imply that Christ redeemed the whole world though his death. Colossians 2:15 and 1 John 3:8 claim Christ's victory over all sin, death, and powers. Consider for a moment that if not everyone for whom Christ died is reconciled to him, then Satan essentially "wins" the desired object of humankind. Aren't we told throughout the pages of Scripture that Christ's death is enough to win the battle, that victory is in the cross? There are also many verses that seem to line up with some kind of ultimate reconciliation (Isaiah 53:11; John 12:32; Rom 5:18–19; Ephesians 1:9–10; Colossians 1:19–20, and 1 Timothy 4:10). So, following this view: after death and judgment, all will eventually be brought to repentance. If God desires all to come to him—and is able—why would there be a cut-off point for any opportunity to repent and be forgiven? Given enough time, wouldn't everyone turn to Christ and be saved (Philippians 2:10–11)?

But there are some difficulties within this view. Out of the three most common views of hell, this one is the most abstract and seems to be built on the complete framework of figurative language. If you take this view, you likely admit that we have no idea how time works, nor the details of punishment or torment. Many will simply appeal to God's nature and sense of justice. Would a Second Temple blasphemer be in a state of weeping or gnashing of teeth longer than someone who passed from this life just before the great judgment? In taking this view, one would need to simply affirm and believe in the justice of God through grace and a timeline we rightly do not understand in our humanity. As you see, this view takes on a bit of a vague understanding. Admittedly, those who hold to this view would simply say that God hasn't revealed the complete plan to us, and that is hard to argue. We clearly don't see the entire unarguable biblical picture yet.

When evaluating this view, some will struggle with the idea that all sin could be eventually reconciled. The question you have to ask is, "In God's omnipotence, could he allow some to experience the qualities of hell and then, eventually, allow all to be reconciled back to him in complete obedience?" Could all of humanity possibly come to these terms in the end? Christian universalism would claim that at some point, no matter how much time it might take, God will win the hearts and minds of everyone.

Many passages lead us to think that in the end, God will reconcile everything to himself. In Romans 5:18 we read that in Adam all die and in Christ all will be made alive. If you consider this carefully, it seems to point to universal salvation. You see, in Adam (which is another word for earthly man) "*all*" will receive physical death. Well, we know this to be inherently true. All humans will die a physical death. Continue this thought with me: if you're going to take "all" to be interpreted as everyone (and it is hard not to), then that would mean that in Christ (who has made us new spiritual creations) everyone would also experience life. Last time I checked, "all" means "all."

What about Revelation 21:25, where it says the gates to the New Jerusalem will always be open? This could be figurative for something else, but it sure seems to suggest that this process of transformation in Jesus will be open or offered forever or until all might come.

One last consideration for universal reconciliation (and even some conditionalist views) is that if you meet Jesus and spend any time in whatever hell might be, who wouldn't turn back to him? We know from the Scriptures that some did, but in a sense of post-throne eschatological judgment, it seems to me that everyone probably would.

Is there ever a time that the offer to join Jesus and his kingdom expires? We typically think of the judgment as being final, but it's quite interesting to think that the Bible actually doesn't tell us that it's the last chance; it just tells us that that's the time we're going to be judged for our actions here on earth. Would God ever prevent a person (or spiritual being) from placing their obedience in him? When Scripture speaks of placing your faithful obedience in Christ, we don't ever read about a cap on it. I think you will be surprised when you study what the Bible actually says about time being short.

Truly, this last view is the best right? Wouldn't we all want this? In a way I think all Christians should be hopefulfor the revealed truth to be the Universal Reconciliation view. ! But the question I beg you to dive into is, which one, according to your exegesis, is actually best taught in Scripture?

## Part 5: The Orthodox View of Hell

The last view is called the orthodox view. This view does have its roots in the Bible, as the others do, but it is probably going to be the most abstract or hardest to frame within all of Scripture. We can all agree that even where there is only a glimmer of light surrounded by darkness, we can still find Jesus. Over and over, we read in Scripture that love is a choice but people have to choose it. So, in this thinking, your condition or understanding of hell will be framed by your condition of God. The very love of God is what lights up the fires of heaven and hell. Some will immediately understand this framework while others reading are already lost.

If God's presence is a consuming fire, then perhaps the descriptions of hell are suggesting the same location or dominion found in the story of Lazarus, which hades and Abraham's bosom seem to describe from an old covenant context. Some will react differently to the consuming fire. In other words, what if everyone goes to the same place but *interprets* it differently. Your experience will be blissful if you are in relationship with God, but those who are in a state of rejection of God will experience the same place as unending torment. All are in a forever state, but it is construed as more figurative in terms of your experience within this state.

An orthodox understanding of hell would say that when the Bible describes a river or perhaps a fiery place, those who are with God would view this as joy in a wonderful place, while those who are not with God somehow experience the same thing as torment.

God's inescapable love is the very thing that will torment them. Essentially, the torment of hell becomes remorse. In the same way, God himself is paradise for the saints, and God himself is hell for those that refuse to accept his refining fire. Many Scriptures speak to the fact that Christ has reconciled himself to humankind as God. It is man who has opposed himself to God.

One of the main differences of an orthodox understanding of heaven and hell compared to the other views is that there is no separation from God. As this can make sense from the framework that all will eventually meet their maker . . . from my perspective this is the most problematic issue for the orthodox understanding of hell. Throughout Scripture we read about God being separated from man.

Another issue to work through with the orthodox view of hell is the problems associated with the righteous knowing the unrighteous are in torment in the same place. It would be difficult for me to be in joy knowing that my loved ones are in torment. This plays into ETC views as well. Revelation tells us that there will be no more sorrow or death or pain. In our human thinking, these views of heaven and hell are difficult to reconcile.

Any view is going to require study and personal exegesis, and each person needs to come to their own position through faithful contemplation and prayer.

## Part 6: Hell in Conclusion

Most people are surprised when they approach Scripture within an unbiased framework to find out what it really says. All of these views are actually not far away from the next, and none of them are heretical, as people assume they might be when encountering them for the first time. The goal of this writing is to function as a launch pad for the reader to fall in love with the Word and learn to thoroughly enjoy the journey as they grow closer to God. Let's summarize some of our thoughts on hell within this understanding.

When it really comes down to it, the difference between annihilation and eternal conscious torment is that one continues to go on in a never-ending cycle of torment and the other has finality. The eternal torment camp likes to take Revelation 14:11 and show the language of the smoke going up forever and forever as the main proof passage for eternal conscious torment. But the smoke rising can simply mean that they've been consumed. In Scripture, fire often has a terminal implication, but it also regularly carries refining implications (symbolizing the divine presence and power of God), which also will play into the orthodox view and the Old Testament foreshadowing within all of them. When we die, we stand before the pure, undiluted love of God that's described as insatiable fire. Perhaps the work of sanctification on earth is finished or made more complete as God purifies what is compatible within his presence and burns up everything that is not, allowing many to eventually be in the presence of God's holiness. We see this understanding more within an orthodox or universal reconciliation understanding of hell, but it possibly fits into the conditionalist approach too. Many believe that in the presence of God all will be made full (*teleioó*). If something is not in conformity with the holiness of God, it will either be made full or will be released as the chaff in the wind (Hebrew metaphor for returning to the earth.) With universal reconciliation, all may eventually be made full. In conditionalist thinking, God may withdraw the gift of existence from those that are not compatible with the kingdom; but similarly, some may also enter God's presence based on a measure of grace given after life on this earth. In this way, life withdrawn from Eden as the first death simply foreshadows the second death of those that are not compatible. If they can't be reconciled in this life or the next, then they will cease to exist by the hand of God.

Jesus warns everyone that their actions on earth will produce consequences *both in this life and the next*. As an example, one of Jesus's teachings most frequently associated with hell is Matthew 25:46, where the Greek word *aionios* is translated as "eternal" (in "eternal punishment") but could be rendered as "occurring in a future age," which could work within any of these views. It is also worth noting that "eternal punish-*ment* as a noun" is different than "eternal punish*ing* as a verb." Within the context of the Greek language and the Hebrew thought framework, arguments can be made several different ways within most of the Scriptures and context that we have on hell.

My point is, that if you're truly unbiased in this conversation, Revelation 14 and most other passages on hell really don't determine the debate. It comes down to a personal conviction or framework for your view of all Scripture. In basketball some who study the game think it is won with offense, while others suggest that defense wins the game. Maybe hell is variable in the same way and maybe it isn't. Maybe one day we will find out who is right. The good news is that those who place allegiant faith in God while on this earth need not be worried. Their eternal destiny is a covenant given to us as we walk the journey in the light of Jesus.

Still many believers seek the truth, and should, as children of light. Most believers in annihilation and eternal conscious torment reject any kind of salvation or continued chance of reuniting a person to the presence of God after the great judgment, which is the main difference between those frameworks and ultimate restoration, which sees the continued grace of God offering the possibility for continued eternal life after judgment within the presence of God. Those within the annihilation camp that believe a chance still exists are oftentimes considered to be more universalist (in terms of hell) by the rest of the annihilation camp.

So where do I land? When I look at the totality of Scripture and apply a socio-rhetorical hermeneutic to all of them (a tenet of biblical theology), I don't arrive securely at any one view. I see them a little bit like Scot McKnight describes the golf club bag of atonement theories. Perhaps there is a framework by which they might all make sense that is beyond our earthly comprehension. Since I tend to go with answers that seem to be the most clearly defined by Scripture, I find myself needing to define death as death and therefore feel that some perspective of annihilation makes the most sense. I would love it if in the end God reconciles all, so I may be a hopeful universalist, but I find myself having a hard time putting it all together within this lens of Scripture. I find myself leaning toward more figurative usage of eschatological terms but also firmly believe in the physical existence of a lake of fire. I don't see much merit for the traditional view of eternal conscious torment within Scripture. I think it is based far more on Greek mythology and tradition than anything else.

> I would love to see everyone reconciled to Christ—after all, that is our primary directive as Christians, right? Let's remember that in him, all things are possible. According to

> the nature of God, annihilation seems to fit better than eternal conscious torment; but in the end God is just regardless of what we think. We may not comprehend the fullness of this in our humanity, but we are asked to live in obedient trust, which gives way to eternal life in the presence of God, and not death. If you are walking with God, luckily most of this conversation is largely irrelevant to your future state. But as we continue to know more of Scripture and what it means, we grow to know Jesus himself.

*YouTube Expedition44 keyword search: Hell*

# CHAPTER 11

# Final Thoughts: This Is the Way

To be in Christ is to be a living exegesis of the narrative of Christ, a new performance of the original drama of exaltation following humiliation, of humiliation as the voluntary renunciation of rights and selfish gain in order to serve and obey.

—Michael J. Gorman, *Cruciformity: Paul's Narrative Spirituality of the Cross*

I grew up playing with Star Wars figures and dreaming of the stars. A generation later, I find myself spending my life enthralled with my children watching reruns, talking theories, and role playing through various intergalactic toys. Star Wars is a saga about the war that wages between forces of good and evil. Although I am not convinced this is intentional, there are a lot of Christian themes and parallels throughout the storyline. Some have accused Lucas of similar Christian sentiments (among many other things, such as presenting an anti-institutional narrative). From a Christians perspective, much of the storyline follows the backward kingdom thinking that we find in the Bible. The "bad guys" of the galaxy, who are rebelling against the established empire, are actually the defenders of what is good and right. The heroes of the story are outsiders, rogues, hermits, and orphans; the least become the greatest within a remnant, ragamuffin kingdom that is often beaten and battered by the prevailing enemy.

The establishment representing what is traditionally good, the Jedi Order, becomes questionably tainted. In many ways this resembles the Pharisees. Eventually, in the later Star Wars storyline, we are led to a realization that the Jedi Order has done nearly as much harm as good. Eventually they need to come to an end. Luke Skywalker plays the part of the savior of the galaxy and is ushered in by the prophets that came before him, who become spirit forms in much the same fashion as Moses and Elijah at the transfiguration. Some even go as far as to interpret Luke's failures with the training the younglings as God's remorse toward a people who continue to walk away from him.

The center of the story is the all-encompassing "Force," which acts as a moral axis. The world likes to view something like this Force as a god. The connection to the Force is often described as strengthened through devotion and perseverance to truly know and understand the depth of its supernatural form. Often there is a battle between the light and the dark, and heroes of the film fall or rise to one side or the other. Redemption is a major theme of the films throughout various plots and stories that all play and build on the overall lens of the narrative. Each movie takes one more step to reveal the complete storyline. The struggle is constant for each character, and all are focused on themes of salvation. Together they join as a unified force to embrace the power within and arise victorious from a seemingly dark universe, finding hope in what has been won for all to find peace that will forever guide.

The latest Disney release, the Mandalorian, continues to play on religious themes. But this time it may hit a bit closer to home—namely, at the heart of American Christianity. It seems to be taking aim at the core of what we have always known. Some grapple with this, equating it to a postmodern questioning of what we have always thought was right. Toward the end of the main Star Wars storyline, we see the Jedi (a picture of traditional church or modern day Pharisees) starting to fade and be questioned. The Jedi were established as the peacekeepers of the galaxy. Was this really the way to peace in the galaxy? In many ways, they seemed to be doing more harm than good.

Most recently, in the Mandalorian TV series, nearly the same question is raised concerning "the way" the Mandalorian has always known and been brought up in. If you aren't familiar with the series, the central figure of the story has been led to believe a certain path was the only way of life since childhood—a belief he is now questioning. At the beginning of the series, you find yourself aligning with this kind of thinking. It must be the way! But as you follow the storyline you begin to find yourself questioning what seemed to be so right. Things are starting to get blurry, and the cause the central figure has devoted his life to doesn't seem to add up anymore. As other perspectives or facts come to surface and you start to see revelation of truth, you become torn. You start to question, "Is this the way?"

The helmet of the Mandalorian signifies the religion he has always known. Yet he is confronted with having to put this aside when he is forced to choose whether to stick with what tradition has always told him is right, or to go with what his spirit says is right. The series finishes with him removing his helmet to say goodbye to "the child," Baby Yoda. We see a story where the central figure literally has offered his own life sacrificially over and over in order that this child might find new life with the Jedi. In doing so, he finds himself having humbly acquired the dark saber, which now gives him a right to rule Mandalore as the king. But none of the other Mandalorians are very excited about this. He doesn't seem to meet their expectations of a king coming to return the kingdom of Mandalore to the glory that they hope for. And that is the finish of the season. There is hope for the coming kingdom, but no one knows exactly how or when it will come. You are left with the idea that the Mandalorians were thinking that redemption would look differently.

I don't really need to say much more (particularly if you are a Star Wars fanatic). If you don't follow, you're probably lost with this storyline anyway! Either way, I think you can probably understand the connections. Today we are all caught up in a world where the traditional teachings, which we were raised to think were truth, seem as messed up as the postmodern world that seeks to steal and corrupt every part of truth within our creed. Everything is mucked up and we are caught in the middle, longing to simply find the way—the love of God within an increasingly dark and desperate world.

The way is clearly Yahweh. The one true God of ancient covenant is only found within the complete context of the Word, revealed in Jesus as Lord. This comes by embarking on a journey that involves a message of hope to all who place their obedient faith in this way of life. To unabashedly pursue holiness to its fullest as a mighty, remnant light bearer who pervades the darkness and gives peace, hope, and love to a lost and dying world. To humbly accept the calling and proclaim the truth, as together we walk in the light of King Jesus, proclaiming his kingdom. That we might bear the actual image and name of Jesus and present ourselves a living sacrifice, set apart to the coming King and kingdom in servanthood within a royal priesthood.

To him be the glory, forever and ever. Amen.

# About the Author

D
r. Will Ryan lives with his family in Lake Geneva, Wisconsin, with his wife Krista of 20 years and counting and 4 beautiful boys named Ty, Will, Kade, and Reid. They enjoy soccer, volleyball, skiing, shooting, and hunting, as well as most anything outside.

Dr. Ryan has a bachelor's degree from Moody Bible Institute, a master's in Curriculum and Instruction and Administration from the University of Wisconsin, and a ThD in biblical Studies from Covenant Theological Seminary (CTS). Dr. Ryan is the head of the Theology and Biblical Studies department at CTS and co-leads a YouTube channel and podcast with Matt Mouzakis called expedition 44, which discusses Scripture.

Printed in the United States
by Baker & Taylor Publisher Services